3 Truths & 7 Mindsets

Changing the way we think to experience Jesus' promise of 'abundant' peace, joy and purpose

Peter Bourke

Dedication

To my grandchildren - I pray every day that you will grasp God's truth and embrace healthy, Jesus-centered mindsets that equip you to experience a profound sense of peace, joy and purpose that will be a light for others in your life.

Contents

Introduction

There's a paradox I've struggled to fully understand – why are so many generally successful people, including faith-minded people, consumed with worry, struggling to find genuine happiness, and restless with their sense of purpose in life? Is there something we're missing?

What do you want more of in life?

If you could say in one word what you want more of in life, what would it be?

A columnist at Forbes magazine, Kathy Caprino, asked her followers this precise question a few years ago and for the nearly 800 respondents, the eight most commonly mentioned words provide a sense of the human condition – the average person's lament if you will. What would you guess was most prevalent?

Here's what Caprino summarized as the top eight responses, ordered by frequency of mentions:

- Happiness
- Money
- Freedom
- Peace
- Joy
- Balance
- Fulfillment
- Confidence

Ponder this list and you'll likely have questions about what is meant by each. You'll also have a tendency to categorize several of these because they're either related or have significant cause-and-effect relationships.

For example – it's often hard to clearly distinguish the difference between happiness and joy. There are certainly inter-relationships between money, freedom and balance. If I have more money, it's logical to expect that I'd have more freedom about how much I work and even where I work, which would logically improve the balance I experience between work and the rest of my non-work life.

So, if you accept my premise and allow me the liberty to 'bucket' this list of eight core desires, they fit into four logical categories and I'll add a simple, self-assessment question to ponder for each:

- Happiness (we'll include 'joy' here) – Do you feel a pervasive sense of joy in your life?
- Freedom (we'll include 'money' and 'balance' for simplicity) – Do you have the flexibility and resources to do the things you aspire to do and the choice to do them?
- Peace – Do you experience a deep, genuine and sustained peace of mind?
- Purpose (we'll include 'fulfillment' and 'confidence' here) – Do you feel a clear sense of purpose about your life and about the reason you exist?

It's a less-than-perfect categorization but reasonably captures the common laments that I've heard expressed by people from all walks of life with whom I've been privileged to spend time. These noble, one-word aspirations are elusive to most people, even to those that you and I would assess as being successful and accomplished.

We could simplify this even further and argue that happiness is what we most ardently desire. In Blaise Pascal's words: "All men (and women) seek happiness. This is without exception. Whatever different means they use, they all tend to this end. The cause of some going to war, and of others avoiding it, is the same desire in both – to be happy. This is the very motive of every action of everyone. Even of those who hang themselves."

Just about every decision you've made today was done with happiness in mind: the meals you've eaten, the clothes you put on this morning, and even turning up the hot water in the shower for five extra minutes. Your happiness is more than just a feeling. Science and medicine have increasingly proven that our happiness impacts our health, our relationships and even our success – for better or for worse.

The central aim of this book is to provide a simple, powerful set of principles to bridge the gap in experiencing these most-desirable aspirations. I'll contend that a genuine sense of joy, peace, freedom and purpose are yours to experience regardless of your talents, your bank account, or even your current circumstances. Your ability to experience them is less about what you know and far more about how you think (our mindsets) and what you believe (our truths).

Why are these attributes elusive?

They're elusive in part because they can't be pursued as an outcome. It's fruitless to resolve to "find happiness" because happiness is an end result, not a 'thing' to chase. Retired Pastor and Author Tim Keller explains the pursuit of happiness (and righteousness) in this way, "If you seek righteousness first, you get happiness. If you seek happiness first, you get neither." It's a bit like saying, "I'm going to pursue being wealthy!" It's futile as a pursuit in and of itself. Instead, you'll have to make the requisite investments of your time, energy, and resources in a career or business venture to ultimately achieve the "wealthy" outcome you aspire to achieve.

There are a few other prominent factors that make things like our peace of mind and our happiness elusive:

Life is hard – It's hard for a myriad of reasons; some of which are beyond your control, while others are self-imposed. We've all had to come to grips with the reality that we're going to suffer bumps and bruises in our lives. As the popular national insurance company commercial was famous for highlighting a few years back: "life comes at you fast!"

Do any of these trials and tribulations sound familiar in your life?

- Sometimes we're just dealt some bad hands – an accident, an illness, a stock market crash, a job loss, or countless other adverse events that you've likely experienced.
- Life just isn't 'fair' – It's easy to feel as though we deserve at least equitable treatment in life. In reality, we're not promised, or provided anything close to fair and equitable – particularly in our highly-biased personal opinion. Some people are more skilled, others are better looking, and yet others are just luckier than the rest of us.
- We don't always make wise decisions – and like it or not, our decisions usually determine our path and trajectory in life. Consider the decisions you've made in the past about friendships, investments, or even career-related choices... would you be better off if you had the opportunity to turn the clock back and make different choices in some of these areas?
- We live in a broken, imperfect world – imperfect people, dysfunctional institutions, and even the

4

occasional natural disasters all contribute to challenging and compromising our personal well-being.

Unrealistic expectations – Consciously or not, we all carry unrealistic expectations. Stop and ponder your expectations – do you expect things to go your way in general? If something doesn't go well, how do you tend to react? Disappointed? Angry? Or downright demoralized?

Perhaps it's our pride that makes these disappointments more difficult, or maybe it's an innate sense that we're entitled to have mostly good things happen to us. When they don't, we feel we've been cheated in some way.

The reason our expectations matter so much is that they profoundly impact our happiness. I ran across a video recently that featured Gary Smalley, a well-known author of numerous books on marriage and relationships. He was discussing contentment and he talked about a time a few years previously when he was struggling and dissatisfied with life and he was introduced to a simple equation for happiness. Happiness, he said, is the gap between our expectations in life and our reality. When the gap is large in important personal areas of life (our career, our financial status, or our marriage for examples), we are likely to be unhappy.

If you wrestle with this concept, there's only two ways to close the gap: you can substantially improve your current reality (not always easy to do) or you can let go of or lower some of your expectations. In Smalley's case, he became determined to surrender his unrealistically-high expectations to God – and it profoundly, and positively impacted his happiness.

What about you? What do you expect from your job? From your spouse? From your children? From yourself? Or even from God? These expectations will significantly impact your happiness, either positively or negatively, as we'll further explore in this book.

We struggle with our purpose and our calling - Henry David Thoreau contended that most people live much of their adulthood in "quiet lives of desperation." Perhaps Thoreau puts his finger on the struggle that so many have with the meaning of life...or lack thereof. Am I here for a purpose? If so, what am I "called" to do? The fact that Rick Warren's book, *The Purpose Driven Life* is one of the best-selling, non-fiction books in history demonstrates that this struggle to find purpose is a shared human affliction

When we don't feel or understand our sense of purpose, life feels like a never-ending treadmill and that race will eventually exhaust us.

The mind is a dangerous thing - If we're not careful about how and what we think about, our minds are almost naturally preoccupied with negative fears and worries. We're our own worst enemies in this regard. Worry is so natural and prevalent in today's world that it seems almost normal. We worry about the past – which we can do nothing about. We worry about the future – most of which will not actually occur. We even worry about what others think about us and quickly fall prey to the comparison trap. So much of our preoccupation with worry is focused on things we actually have very little ability to control.

Why are we so prone to allow our mind to engage in counter-productive thoughts and worries? Why do we obsess about outcomes with which we have very little control? Is it our excessive self-reliance? Or could it be our lack of genuine faith and trust in God and His sovereignty?

We'll aim to address these questions and more.

Our faith...or lack thereof

6

You might assume that a faith-filled person doesn't struggle in experiencing elusive desires like peace and happiness. But if our faith isn't translated into our conscious, day-to-day activities and relationships, it's become more theoretical than 'applied.'

Why else wouldn't a person with a strong faith experience plenty of peace and happiness? Perhaps in part because we tend to compartmentalize our faith as separate from the rest of our life 'compartments.' "Yes, I believe in God, but I still have bills to pay and God doesn't write the checks!" Or, "Yes, I go to church every week but I don't really know how to integrate God into my relationships, my financial decisions, and my other daily priorities."

We're all prone to being faith-filled, Jesus-followers who still fall victim to endless worrying, the trap of comparing ourselves to others, and making choices and decisions that all contribute to feeling as though something is profoundly missing in our life. Author Dallas Willard makes this point better than anyone: "We don't believe something by merely saying we believe it, or even when we believe we believe it. We believe something when we *act* as if it were true."

Jesus made it clear in John's Gospel that He wants us to live life to the fullest and with a genuine sense of peace, joy, and purpose. He called it the abundant life: *I came that they may have life, and have it abundantly* (John 10:10).

If we truly aspire to this 'abundant' life that Jesus promised, how do we close the chasm between these often-elusive aspirations and our current reality? The answer is found in our mindsets. We literally get to <u>choose</u> how we think (our mindsets) and how we respond to our circumstances. And it's these choices that will make the biggest difference in our ability to experience the abundant sense of joy, peace, and purpose to which we aspire.

When "what we want" is elusive

If we have a reasonable amount of clarity on the short list of one-word answers that we most desire to have more of, why don't we just clench our teeth and make it happen? Isn't it just a matter of personal commitment and resolve? Or is it something else?

Here are a few 'go to' strategies we tend to employ and then I'll offer a mindset-related suggestion:

Grin and bear It – In essence, this strategy is to "suck it up and stay the course." "I can't really change my lot in life, so why try?" It's a defeatist mindset and strategy that far too many choose and it most-often leads to a sense of resignation. It's also far from satisfying and yet may be the most common strategy employed.

Self-medicate – For some, the best way to overcome hurt and disappointment is to escape reality. This is one reason why addictive behaviors like drugs, alcohol, and even pornography are so common today. "At least I have an escape from my pain and disappointment." Self-medicating behaviors may indeed offer a temporary reprieve from pain, but they won't fill the void in a substantial or sustained way.

Work harder; achieve more – This was my strategy for far too many years. I'll grant that working harder is a noble and well-intentioned strategy, but it's most often undermined by the challenging realities of life and unrealistic expectations that were outlined above. "If I work harder...and make more money...I'll have more freedom...and more balance...and ultimately experience more peace and happiness!"

Sounds simple...but still elusive. Famous philosopher (and comedian) Jim Carrey said it well: "I wish everyone could get rich and famous and accomplish everything they ever dreamed of so they can see that's not the answer."

If these strategies aren't working, maybe something else entirely is required...

Change your Mindsets – This is what we'll explore for the balance of this book. You and I can consciously <u>choose</u> to change the way we think and therefore how we respond to things that happen in our lives each and every day.

We'll explore three 'truths' and seven 'mindsets' that offer the greatest potential for helping us to live with a genuine sense of meaning and purpose; experiencing a resilient joy that isn't extinguished by adverse circumstances; and enjoying an intimacy with God that most struggle to achieve and sustain.

This is the journey I've been on for nearly two decades now – transitioning from the workaholic, Type "A" person who was intent to solve all of my problems by working hard and accomplishing everything I set out to do, mostly by self-will and maximum effort, to a Jesus-follower who embraces a small, healthier and more liberating set of truths and mindsets that are life-giving.

I'm still a work in process and I'm certain that I'll continue to be an imperfect example for as long as I'm privileged to be alive in this world. But even the process of understanding, testing and embracing these mindsets is providing me with a taste of what intimacy with God is all about. I'd like to invite you on the journey with me...

These truths and mindsets won't change the person you are or what you know or where you came from. You'll still have the same talents, the same likes and dislikes, and generally speaking, the same current circumstances. What will change, for your benefit, is how you think and how you view your world

– especially the less-than-perfect world you occupy today. They'll change your paradigms and your perspectives. And they have the greatest potential to allow you to experience the peace, joy and purpose that each of us are so desperately seeking.

The Power of Our Mindsets

...and the Lies that Distort Them

Like it or not, you are either a victim or beneficiary of your dominant mindsets. These mindsets are powerful because they dictate most of what we do, what we think, and even who we are. And many of these mindsets are subconscious - sourced from our childhood, our friends, our family, and even our social surroundings.

We all have them, although we don't take much time to consciously consider them. The narcissist's mindset is pretty obvious, "I'm not only the center of my universe, I'm also the center of THE universe." Someone with little self-confidence has a very different mindset: "I don't really feel capable of accomplishing much so I'd rather not even try."

They are so innate that we often don't understand what they are and how they affect us. Have you ever taken the time to consider what your mindsets sound like? Are they positive in nature, or mostly self-defeating?

Here are a few additional examples, both positive and negative, of that small voice in our heads that can profoundly determine our paradigms and our paths:

- "I'm entitled to _____." (fill in the blank here – a better car? A better job? A better husband? Or...something else?)
- "I don't deserve even what I have."
- "I deserve to be happy."
- "I need to leave a legacy before I die."

11

- "I've got to take personal responsibility for my life - and my success is entirely up to me."
- "I've got to fight for what I deserve."
- "Those that work the hardest, win!"
- "I'll never be more successful."
- "I can survive in life without help from other people."
- "I'm just grateful for the blessings that God has already provided."

These mindsets aren't just limited to how we view ourselves. They can apply to your view of your family, your 'tribe,' or even your country. Take the United States as an example – there's a reasonable portion of our population with a growing view that the United States is a dishonorable country with a dishonorable past. While we have a flawed history of slavery and racial inequality (as two such notable examples), it lacks nuance to conclude that we are therefore an ignoble country. What if we allow our mindset on this topic to consider the good along with the bad, leading to a less extreme, more balanced view?

The mindsets you choose, on this topic or countless others, will impact your relationships, your attitudes, and even your health (physically and mentally). Even your joy and your peace of mind are dependent less on what you know and significantly more on how you think – which is what our mindsets are all about.

What is a mindset?

Think about a mindset as the ingrained thought 'filter' you have on everything from the mundane to the strategic. Allow me to illustrate:

If your watch breaks, it can be traumatic for the person whose mindset places a high level of importance on their watch (especially the expensive smart watches that alert you to text and email messages!). This will never be an issue for me because I wear a $30 Timex watch. I consider my watch a disposable commodity and when (not if) it breaks, I'll go find a suitable (and inexpensive) replacement. It doesn't impact my productivity, my attitude, or my happiness in the least.

On the strategic end of the spectrum – what if you unexpectedly become unemployed? Your mindset related to your job/career will likely matter significantly more. Some would even consider a job loss as catastrophic, especially if their identity is wrapped up in their career or if they believe that this setback could severely impact their future career prospects and their financial security.

With a healthier mindset about your career, you'd look at your career transition as a challenge but not a crisis. Sure, there's work to be done and you'll be thoughtful and diligent about landing the next job. But you also accept that the time it takes to become re-employed is not entirely in your control. In essence, you'll do your best, but when and where you become re-employed is not entirely in your control.

Our mindsets are a compilation of many things: our view of 'truth' (more on that topic to come); our expectations (that often evolve over time); the strength and conviction of our faith and trust in the sovereignty of God; and by our physical, emotional and relational health (particularly the deep, intimate relationships that give us a genuine sense of being loved).

Why our mindsets matter?

Mindsets dictate so much of who we are and what we do but they also profoundly impact our sense of joy and well-being. Popular Ted Talk™ speaker and author, Shawn Achor, is a self-professed expert researcher on happiness and his entire premise supports this notion: our happiness is largely dictated by the conscious choices we make and the habits we form that change the way we think.

Our mindsets also determine our response to adverse situations. They profoundly affect our attitude – either positively or negatively – about today and about our future. They'll provide us with hope or represent an anchor of hopelessness. They even dictate whether we sleep soundly at night and when dawn breaks a few hours later, whether we even want to get out of bed the next morning.

I'm intentionally over-emphasizing that our mindsets are conscious choices we each make. We can literally <u>choose</u> healthy mindsets regardless of our circumstances, our skillsets, our bank account balance, or even our history. I'm not minimizing the value or importance of therapy and counseling related to past trauma and experiences – these provide great value. But even with the benefit of effective counseling, we each have the ability to choose how we think.

It's precisely why two people in the same circumstances can view life with entirely different mindsets – one whose perspective is positive and hope-filled; the other whose circumstances feel dire and hopeless. The difference lies in their mindsets and in their expectations.

When your mindsets aren't aligned with God's truth and His promises, they're most-often debilitating and self-defeating. Here are two examples from the perspective of a person with a distorted truth (from a faith perspective) that negatively shapes their mindsets and ultimately their outlook on life:

- "My past sins can't possibly be forgiven and I'll have to carry the guilt and shame forever."
- "There is no existence beyond our life here on planet Earth and therefore our lives are relatively meaningless."

On the other hand, a person who adopts healthy, faith-centered truths that support an entirely different mindset might instead believe:

- "Yes, I'm imperfect and prone to sin, but I rest in the truth that my sins are entirely forgiven and I can relish the freedom from guilt and shame that this promise provides."
- "My hope rests in God's promise that my eternal future is secure."

Do you get a sense of how crucial the difference between these disparate paradigms will be on our outlook about life? Or how crucial our view of the truth (and therefore our mindset) is to our perspectives and countenance? It's literally (and figuratively) the difference between light and dark.

The lies we tell ourselves that distort our mindsets

I had the privilege of spending some time recently with a dear friend who is a small business owner. The challenge he invited me to wrestle with is that the business he owns and the ministry work he does leaves him feeling fulfilled, on one hand, but often simultaneously feeling overwhelmed and out of gas.

Does that sound at all familiar to you?

So "Patrick" invited me to better understand his business, his clients, and his goals to see if we could come up with a few ideas that could help him better approach his business and his client-service model in order to create a better, healthier balance in his life.

As we dug into the discussion, I think Patrick was hoping for some innovative 'silver bullet' ideas on time management or a few tactics to make all of this work better. What we both realized in the course of our discussions is that the problem had less to do with tactics and time management, and far more to do with his mindsets about his roles, commitments, and obligations.

Specifically, Patrick had embraced some lies and mindsets that proved debilitating. When we allow that to happen, it can actually be self-destructive. Here are a few examples of some common, unhealthy lies we sometimes believe:

- "I'm obligated to accomplish everything (tasks, clients, etc.) that comes my way."
- "I can't say "no" and run the risk of disappointing people that rely on me or that I care about."
- "If I don't help/serve people who need help I'm not being a good friend."
- "I can't let people see me rest or relax or they won't think highly of me."
- And perhaps the most dangerous of all, "I am indispensable – and things won't get done (or done right) without me."

Can you think of other lies that you're sometimes guilty of embracing? Do you recognize that these lies can cause you to stay in the wrong job or fuel your workaholism? It's this tension and these lies that prevent us from adopting helpful mindsets and ultimately lead us to make poor choices that steal our joy and our peace. Patrick and I had to struggle with what the corresponding truths looks like. The "truths" that God designed for those who follow Him look entirely different.

Using Patrick's examples, here are some truths that proved helpful: God wants us to rest in the truth that our identity as His follower gives us the knowledge and assurance that our satisfaction and our joy is eternal, not subject to the judgment and opinion of others. God calls us to use our skills and talents for the benefit of others but to do so with balance – so that

16

serving others is both useful and sustainable. And perhaps more than anything, God wants our hearts, not our endless task-orientation. Jesus made it crystal clear in the sermon on the mount: *Seek first His kingdom and His righteousness and all these other things will be provided to you as well* (Matt 6:33).

When we embrace these truths and principles, our mindsets are often polar-opposite of the lies outlined above. They're also foreign to those who find themselves overwhelmed and over-committed on the treadmill we call 'life.' Here are some examples that Patrick and I landed on that proved transformational and that highlight the life-giving contrast:

- You are valuable, but not indispensable! I'm sorry to deliver the news that if you died tomorrow, those in your orbit would be sad for a few weeks (or days) and then we'd all figure out how to survive without you (how's that for brutal honesty?). A lot of the lies listed above are centered on a false belief about our self-importance and this belief alone puts pressure on us that God didn't intend.
- You have the ability, and the authority, to decide what you'll do with your finite time and energy and to <u>choose</u> where (and with whom) you'll spend your time – not an obligation to serve anyone who happens to find you or pursue you. How much more balance (and sanity) would you have in your life if you felt empowered to <u>choose</u> the people and tasks that best leverage your personal gifts and talents? Most of us have more of this ability than we may think.
- You don't have to be available 24/7. The more reactive we are to those who want our time, the less intentional we are in using our talents in the most effective ways. Embrace some boundaries in your time/calendar that

allow you to <u>choose</u> how and when you'll allocate your valuable, yet finite time.

- Rest and relaxation are life-giving and renewing for all of us and God designed rest (including the weekly Sabbath) from the beginning of our existence.
- And finally, to do all of this well, you have to proactively decide what you're going to <u>stop</u> doing. The only way you'll have time to focus on the right priorities is if you determine what you won't do anymore. This is often the most difficult mindset and discipline of all!

What about you? Are there some lies you've embraced that are contrary to God's design and that are compromising your healthy mindsets? It may be time to have someone in your circle of friends help you decipher the truth from the lies you've embraced over time. Paul gives us clarity on how to handle the unhealthy lies that can dominate us: *...take captive every thought to make it obedient to Christ* (2 Cor 10:5). Devoting time to this effort will be life-giving - the 'abundant' life that Jesus promises.

Secular vs. Faith-centered mindsets

I've studied books and resources about mindsets for several years and I'd put most into two classic categories – the personal/professional (which represents the majority) and the faith-centered. The former are most-often focused on mindsets that will equip a person to be "successful." Of course, the definition of success varies greatly. Most focus on career success, financial success, or even success in relationships, all of which are important and valuable.

On the other hand, the success orientation will be less satisfying for those of who are faith-centered and who believe that what really matters in life is beyond what we experience in the few decades we're fortunate enough to exist here on Earth. Our source of satisfaction (or lack thereof) is less about worldly success and achievements and far more about the journey to answer the transcendent questions that God put in our personal 'operating system' like... "Why do I exist?" Or, "What's my purpose/calling?"

Here's the way author Dallas Willard characterized what really matters: "The main thing God gets out of your life is not the achievements you accomplish. It's the person you become."

There are countless people who are self-professed and committed Jesus-followers whose inherent mindsets still allow them to be dominated by worry and fear, not the peace and joy that our faith promises and that most aspire to experience. I'm sure we all know some faith-filled people who face challenges and setbacks in life and struggle to deal with these challenges because of dominant, negative mindsets. It's a paradox: on one hand they can believe that God supernaturally created them and that His son, Jesus, came supernaturally to live amongst us and died for the forgiveness of our sins. And on the other hand, they can still be dominated by fear and worry because they lack faith and trust in God's goodness and His sovereignty in their circumstances.

Even with a strong faith, we can't really be the "branch" that is fully attached and nourished by God's "vine" without healthy mindsets (John 15:5). We also can't be the vessels that God designed us to be - vessels that allow Jesus to work in and through us as we bring His love to the waiting world, without healthy mindsets (2 Tim 2:21). Living with genuine joy and peace isn't just a "nice-to-have," it's an act of worship and a powerful testimony to God's goodness. We can't experience or exude this joy and peace that God promises us without the benefit of healthy, Christ-centered mindsets (John 14:27).

And therein lies the purpose for this simple book. It's not aiming to help you achieve success in the secular world, although I pray that God will walk with you even in that journey. Instead, it's focused on identifying the simple, faith-centered mindsets that draw us closer to intimacy with God and equip us to experience the abundant life that Jesus came and sacrificed to provide us.

Mindsets are a choice!

"Can we *really* choose our mindsets?" you may ask.

I'll defer again to Dallas Willard for his wisdom on this question: "The ultimate freedom we have as human beings is the power to select what we will allow or require our minds to dwell upon."

Life is full of choices and choice may be the biggest freedom we each possess. Too often we have the mistaken belief that we just have to accept the hand we've been dealt in life. It's just not so. Our lives are full of choices we are privileged to make. We get to choose the person we are going to marry. We also then get to choose whether we're going to love that spouse well – regardless of how annoyed we may become with their idiosyncratic habits!

We can choose to not worry about a son or daughter who is going off to college for the first time – if we have the right mindsets. We can choose to forgive a friend who has hurt us – if we have the right mindsets. We can choose to be generous, to love someone who seems unlovable, and to accept hardships as an opportunity to grow – if we have the right mindsets. Healthy mindsets allow us to leverage this freedom of choice to chart the right course for our lives.

You'll find that the strength and conviction of your mindsets tend to grow over time. It's part of our growth journey. When you initially adopt a mindset, it can be easily challenged and tested by trials that arise. With time, and as you grow in the conviction of your faith and trust in God, your mindsets actually become more fortified.

So, if we have a choice about our mindsets, which mindsets are most useful and healthy? And how does this all fit within our faith walk for Christians?

Our truths and our mindsets profoundly impact our path, our trajectory, and even our joy but choosing healthy mindsets doesn't simply depend on your knowledge of God. They require you to *trust* God – His sovereignty, His goodness, and His love for you. Do you trust God with your circumstances? With your children? With your finances? Even with your relationships?

Your faith and belief in God are what gives you the confidence to trust Him. Jesus came to give us life, and to have it abundantly (John 10:10) – and experiencing this abundant life depends on us trusting God with our life and with our future.

Your mindsets will either ignite or extinguish your faith. A strong faith plagued by unhealthy mindsets will lead to discouragement – because you're still prone to be negatively impacted by the circumstances and the challenges that are bound to occur in your life. On the other hand, the person with healthy mindsets and a strong faith will find that even amongst adverse circumstances, their faith and confidence in God is a reliable and growing source of comfort.

This faith and confidence in God will foster a deep, intimate connection with God because He's then *in* your circumstances and *in* your relationships, not compartmentalized in the "God-box" we tend to artificially create. The Jesus-follower who experiences this deep, genuine connection with God is the one best equipped to love others and to be the 'light' we're called to be in this world (Matt 5:16).

21

You and I have the ability to joyfully rise above the fray of everyday turmoil, tensions and events by trusting that our good and loving God, the creator of all things, is bigger and more sovereign than today's tasks and trials. Jesus has made a profound and irresistible promise: "I have told you these things, so that in me you may have peace. In this world you will have trouble. But take heart! I have overcome the world" (John 16:33). We just have to decide to accept and embrace this promise.

God has blessed Devonie and I with the gift of seven grandchildren (so far). Most of them are too young to fully grasp these principles but they are the original reason for this book. They, and all of us for that matter, have the ability to thrive in this increasingly challenging and far-less-than-perfect world. We can be a light in this world if we embrace the right truths and mindsets that we'll explore in the balance of this book. I pray that you and others might benefit from considering the degree to which these principles align with yours.

Discussion Questions

- What one word best describes what you want more of in life?
- Do you believe that Mindsets are a choice? Why, or why not?
- Are there one or two people in your life that seem to have generally healthy mindsets? Can you identify a few of their specific mindsets?
- What are some examples of your own negative mindsets that you sometimes notice?
- What are some examples of healthy mindsets that are prevalent for you?
- What is the most difficult part of embracing new mindsets for you?

Recommended Activity

Ask one or two people who know you best (and whom you trust to share honestly) what they would say about your mindsets...both healthy and unhealthy ones that they've noticed.

3 Truths...

"You can live opposite of what you profess, but you cannot live opposite of what you believe"

Dallas Willard

There are a core set of truths that, by necessity, underlie our knowledge, behavior and even our mindsets. The dictionary defines truth as, "that which is true in accordance with fact or reality." Think of our truths as those things that we believe unfailingly. The sun will rise again tomorrow. Gravity will keep me planted on the ground today. We will all die eventually. You get the picture.

But some truths require us to examine and wrestle with our faith (a belief in what is not seen) because they aren't indisputably provable. Do you believe that our world was created in one big accidental, big bang moment? Or do you believe that all of this (and us) were breathed into existence by a Creator (God)? Where you land on this question will profoundly shape your entire view of your existence, your purpose, and even (or especially) your future. It's this stark contrast that makes it important to begin this discussion of healthy mindsets by aligning on a short list of critical truths that we, as Jesus-followers, not only believe are true but more importantly, *act* as if they are true. These truths fundamentally support any discussion of the seven mindsets that we'll explore in the subsequent chapters of this book.

Over many years I've had a habit of capturing the Bible verses that the Holy Spirit has used to most significantly shape my understanding of God and His call on my life. I've documented these in a small journal that has become my favorite way to study God's Word because these verses are the ones God has used most impactfully for my benefit. In the same vein, I'll share with you the select few verses that best clarify and reinforce each of the three Truths and seven Mindsets. You will undoubtedly find additional scripture verses that God will use for your understanding and I encourage you to proactively seek these scripture verses out in your journey to consciously embrace both truth and healthy mindsets.

Truth #1: Our Creator, God is Real

There's a premise in all of this that is fundamental – do you believe that God is real? If not, the personal and professional mindsets I mentioned previously (i.e., achievement and success) become far more pertinent. Each of us have the privilege to literally decide – is God real? If he isn't, and our existence is an extraordinary coincidence, then many of the mindsets I'll offer become far less relevant. They'll still make your life better, and make you better at life but they'll be far less "strategic" in the scheme of things if God didn't create you and I. On the other hand, if God is real, and He created us and all that exists, then nothing matters more.

Are we an accident?

For me personally, it's impossible to believe that the world we occupy is an accident. Between its delicate balance of size, gravity, oxygen, polarity, and perfect, repeatable orbits; the stunning beauty of nature; and perhaps most convincingly, the incredible miracle of human life itself, how could this world possibly be a random, coincidental occurrence? I can't walk a single day as an observer of all that we're surrounded by and genuinely believe that this was the result of a 'big bang' accident millions of years ago.

So, yes, I believe in the truth that God exists and that He created you and I and all that we inhabit. He is the Creator, and we are the created.

The centerpiece of His creation is the relationship He desires with us since we're the only form of life that He created in His image and with a body, soul, conscience, and even a spirit designed for relationship with Him and with other people.

When are you most in awe of God?

I know this seems like a really elementary question but humor me: stop and ponder for a minute when God is most obvious to you. Or said another way, when are you most in awe of our Creator, God?

...when you see a new born baby who transforms from two disparate single cell contributions belonging to her parents and in the course of 40 weeks becomes a living, breathing, human with an incredibly complex anatomy including a super-computer we call the human brain?

...or when you witness, first-hand, one of nature's stunning creations like the Grand Canyon or Niagara Falls, or... (what are your first-hand examples)?

...or when a song captures your heart and your spirit in a unique way?

...or when you realize the grace and forgiveness God fathomed and embodied in Jesus' birth, death and resurrection more than 2000 years ago for our salvation?

...or when you see random people make extraordinary sacrifices for the benefit of other people they don't even know...and for no personal benefit?

...or (for me anyway) when I get to enjoy a bowl of my favorite ice cream – the perfect and most addictive of all desserts?

...or, maybe God is most obvious to you on a special occasion when you're able to spend time with your family or those you most love?

People commonly ponder why God doesn't perform miracles anymore or why he doesn't talk to us in tangible ways as He did throughout biblical history. In reality, God makes Himself obvious in countless ways that we either miss or take for granted and we overlook these "God winks" that are right in front of us. I recently heard a silent retreat director exhort that we need to find God in all things. That is certainly true but you have to *look* for God to find Him in anything.

Whether your best evidence is from my list above, from your own personal favorites or simply represents a personal leap of faith, consciously choose and then celebrate the first truth that God is real and we have the privilege of being an integral part of God's masterful creation and design. We also have the honor of waking each day as witnesses and instruments of His bigger 'story' as it is revealed to us each day throughout the rest of our lives.

There are three prominent scripture verses that I lean on to reinforce this truth and they provide clarity about God and His creation:

- *In the beginning God created the heavens and the earth* (Gen 1:1)
- *Be still and know that I am God* (Ps 46:10)
- *Yet for us there is one God, the Father, from whom are all things and for whom we exist, and one Lord, Jesus Christ, through whom are all things and through whom we exist.* (1Cor 8:6)

Truth #1: Our Creator, God is Real

Discussion Questions

- What's the most convincing evidence for the existence of God from your perspective?
- When are you most in awe of God and His creation?
- What makes you most doubt the sovereignty of God?
- If you believe that God is real and truly sovereign, how should this change your mindsets, priorities and even your relationships?

Recommended Activity

If a friend asked you, "What's your best evidence that God exists?" How would you answer?

Truth #2: You are Deeply Known and Loved by God

...exactly as you are!

Not only are you created by God (Truth #1) but you're also deeply loved by God – for exactly who and how you are today. Complete with all of your strengths and deficiencies, you are a child of the living God and you've been made uniquely in God's image. For many people, including Jesus-followers, this truth is difficult for us to embrace.

Is it because of our guilt and shame for things we've done in the past? Are we just naturally self-critical? Or is it something else entirely? I'm not confident that I know the answer but I have plenty of evidence that far too many Christians, and even non-Christians who are curious and seeking a relationship with God, get hung up on the notion that God can't possibly love them because of bad choices they've made in the past. It's almost as though we think we're unique in our sinful nature and in our corresponding guilt and shame.

Have you ever met someone for the first time and found yourself quickly marveling at the degree to which they seemingly have their act together in life? Our first and natural tendency is to assume that the people we meet are doing well overall and likely don't face the same challenges or feel the same insecurities that we do.

But when you get beyond the surface level and *really* get to know the people that God puts in your life, you then realize that we're all pretty messy in our own 'special' ways.

This became obvious a few years ago when a close friend of mine and I launched a men's small group through our church comprised of talented, high potential, and faith-filled men that we walked with for a 9-month mentoring program. We met monthly, read challenging books, and even had some deeper, one-on-one meetings with each man. Early on, each of us shared our 'life stories' including our work and family-related challenges in a uniquely transparent way.

Once these men had the opportunity to learn the vulnerable truth about one another, not just the façade we all carefully cultivate, we were all struck by how powerful it was for us to be more fully-known by other faith-filled people in a safe, small-group environment. We also had the opportunity to reflect, by contrast, on how little we really know about the people we see regularly in life – those we work with; those we live near; even those we sit in rows with at church each Sunday.

We assume everyone, other than us, lives a more 'wrinkle-free' life…until we actually get to know the rest of their story. And when we do have the opportunity to go deeper with someone, or even with a few people we can trust, we come to two key realizations: First, that we're not alone in our struggles in life and, second, that we better recognize that the trials and tribulations that have marked our past are often the most strategic events that God has used and will continue to use to shape us into the people He designed us to be.

This second truth, that I pray you'll <u>choose</u> to embrace, is that you can take great comfort in knowing that your past, present, and future are all part of God's masterful design. His aspiration for us is not necessarily to be exceptional (at least by the world's standards), but for us to be humble. Exceptional people are more prone to pride, self-reliance and self-absorption. Humble people, who recognize and even embrace that we're fallible and sinful at our core, are genuinely grateful that we're not only made and loved by God but that we can rest in the notion that His grace assures us that we're forgiven. Humble, faith-filled people who rest in their identity as beloved children of God also have confidence that God will use our mess for good and for His glory.

You were not made to carry the burden of your 'mess' in guilt, in shame, or even by wearing the proverbial 'mask.' Instead, your mess may be exactly what God will use for the benefit of others. He'll use the skills and talents that emerge from that mess to love and minister to others.

Your identity and your worth aren't based on your accomplishment or on the opinion of others. They're determined by the simple and profound truth that you are the beloved child of the Creator, God. The more you're able to embrace this truth, the more freedom you'll experience because you can rest in the notion that God will use you exactly the way He designed you – strengths and weaknesses included!

Perhaps the most compelling evidence of God's love for us is the fact that He sacrificed his son, Jesus, on the cross for the forgiveness of our sins which we'll explore in detail in our third and final truth.

But first, here are a few key scripture verses to reinforce our second truth and that provide clarity about God's relentless, unconditional love for you – precisely as you are:

- *Indeed, the very hairs of your head are all numbered* (Luke 12:7).
- *I will not leave you as orphans; I will come to you* (John 14:18).

32

- *And surely I am with you always to the end of the ages* (Matt 28:20).
- *But He (Jesus) said to me, "My grace is sufficient for you, for my power is made perfect in (your) weakness* (2Cor 12:9-10).
- *For you created my inmost being; you knit me together in my mother's womb. I praise you because I am fearfully and wonderfully made; your works are wonderful, I know that full well* (Ps 139: 13-14).

Truth #2: You are Deeply Known and Loved by God

...exactly as you are!

Discussion Questions

- What parts of your past and even current circumstances seem to be impediments to feeling genuinely loved by God?
- Why is this truth so critical – even before we consider our mindsets?
- How could God possibly love you (or anyone) unconditionally with all of our flaws and imperfections?
- What would change in your behavior and countenance if you truly believe this truth?

Recommended Activities

- Find 5 Bible verses that reinforce this truth for you – and commit your three favorites to memory and reflection for the next three weeks to begin to *"renew"* your mind.
- Ask God to give you a supernatural understanding, comfort and peace about his unconditional love for you...exactly as you are.

Truth #3: Jesus is the Gift of Grace
...that secures your freedom, today and eternally

The most compelling evidence that God loves us so deeply and desires a relationship with you and I is that He sent his son, Jesus, to live here as fully human and fully God. He did so to make Himself "real" to us and now He allows each of us to choose to enter into the relationship he longs to have with us. His love is so profound that Jesus died a brutal, sacrificial death for the freedom from, and the forgiveness for our sins - past, present and future sins.

What's required of us? Only that we're humble enough to choose to accept this gift of grace.

Jesus made this abundantly clear in John's gospel: *For God so loved the world that he gave his one and only Son, that whoever believes in him shall not perish but have eternal life* (John 3:16).

And when we put our faith and trust in Jesus, we become a new creation filled with Jesus' spirit that allows Him to work in and through us to love God and to love the people that God puts in our path.

Through our faith in this final truth about Jesus, God promises us *a peace that surpasses all understanding* (Phil 4:7). More than anything else, I pray that you'll embrace this truth and experience life with Jesus, not apart from Him; a life filled with His peace, regardless of your circumstances; and fully-equipped to share your love and 'light' with others that don't yet understand or embrace these truths.

At the risk of over-simplifying the incredible gift of the gospel: we're each able to decide if God is real and sovereign over this world and when we do, to then decide if we truly trust Him and His goodness. Embracing this truth and making this decision will transform your mindsets...and your life.

If you haven't yet had the opportunity to accept Jesus' gift of salvation, I've included below a simple prayer that I'd encourage you to say or choose your own words from your heart. Here's how you can invite Jesus to be the Lord of your life:

> "Heavenly Father, have mercy on me, a sinner. I believe in you and believe that your word is true. I believe that Jesus Christ is the Son of the living God and that he died on the cross so that I may now have forgiveness for my sins and eternal life. I know that without you, my life is meaningless.
>
> I believe in my heart that you, Lord God, raised Jesus from the dead. Please Jesus, forgive me for every sin I have committed and come into my life as my personal Lord and Savior today. I need you to be my Father and my friend.
>
> I pray this in the name of Jesus Christ. Amen."

If you've taken this step, congratulations! There is no more important decision in your life and I pray that God will make Himself obvious to you as you take some additional steps with scripture, prayer and community to allow you to experience God personally.

Here are a few additional, foundational scriptures that reinforce this third truth and that equip us to adopt healthy mindsets:

- *Come to me, all who labor and are heavy laden, and I will give you rest* (Matt 11:28).
- *And I will ask the Father, and he will give you another advocate to help you and be with you forever...* (John 14 16).
- *No human mind has conceived the things that God has prepared for those who love Him* (1 Cor 2:9).

That's it - three simple, yet profound truths that are fundamental to any of us transforming our mindsets in a Christ-centered way. He created us; we belong to Him because we are deeply loved; and more than anything, God wants an everlasting relationship with you and I and offers to carry our burdens. It's strikingly simple and stunningly profound.

What about you? What are the truths and core mindsets you operate with each day? Have you chosen your narratives or inherited them involuntarily from your childhood or from your social media 'tribe'? Each of us has the freedom, and responsibility, to consciously choose our truths, which will profoundly shape our mindsets.

Truth #3: Jesus is the Gift of Grace
...that secures your freedom, today and eternally

Discussion Questions

- What's the most difficult part of embracing this truth for you?
- Have you taken the profound step to accept the gift of grace and forgiveness that Jesus' death and resurrection offers you? Why or why not?
- What steps could you take to learn more about Jesus and His forgiveness of your sins?
- Once we accept Jesus' gift of grace and forgiveness, what role does the Holy Spirit play in our mindsets?
- What makes this truth liberating for the Jesus-follower?

Recommended Activities

- Join a local Christian church community or Bible study that can help you learn and grow in your faith and relationship with Jesus.
- Pray and ask Jesus to make His presence and His power known to you more personally than ever.

...And 7 Mindsets

Now let's explore the seven mindsets that enable us live the abundant life that Jesus offers us – a life characterized by a deep sense of peace, joy and purpose...regardless of, or perhaps, in spite of our circumstances. To make it easier to remember these key mindsets, I've highlighted a "C" word/phrase in each one that we'll explore in these subsequent chapters:

Mindsets:

1. God is in **Control**...of the outcomes

2. Our **Calling**: Love God & Love Others... with your skills and gifts

3. Becoming **Christ-like**...is a journey

4. **Choose Not to Worry**...it's an imperative, not a suggestion

5. **Choose Humility**...not pride

6. **Choose to Forgive**...sooner than later

7. You're Made for **Community...**don't fly solo

Mindset # 1: God is in Control

...of the outcomes

Do you feel as though you're in control of your life and your future?

It's innate in most of us but it's liberating when you accept and even embrace that you're really not. The good news...God is in control and he can be genuinely trusted with the outcomes in your life and with your future.

On one hand we clamor for control in our lives – control of our circumstances; control of our relationships; even control of our destiny. But with that control comes a huge burden that exists *because* we feel as though we must control everything that happens. Consider the parallel in a business – the CEO of a company technically has control of budgets, resources, priorities, and even the people in an organization, all of which makes him or her feel responsible for the company's results and its future trajectory. And yet, the ultimate success of that organization is largely beyond the CEO's control. The CEO doesn't control the economy, the competitors, their own employee's performance, and even extraneous factors like natural disasters or, God forbid, pandemics.

Now apply this same logic to our lives – yes, there are many things we can and should do to positively impact what we accomplish and where we're headed in life. But the ultimate outcomes are very much out of our control. They depend on timing, relationships, and a myriad of other factors – including a certain degree of luck.

And therein lies the reason we're called in God's word to trust Him with every aspect of our lives, including the unknown outcomes of the future. In essence, because God knows all things, we can rest in the notion that we don't have to know everything.

Embracing this mindset doesn't mean we're promised a problem-free existence – not in the least! But when we learn to trust God and His plans for us, an extraordinary peace is promised. And God's peace is hard to experience in those who feel entirely accountable for everything that happens.

You're not the central actor

I still remember Louie Giglio, a Pastor here in the Atlanta area, preaching more than a decade ago about how we tend to go through life feeling as though we're the central actor in this movie called, "Our Life." Our self-centered perspective tends to believe that the rest of the world – our friends, our work colleagues, our family, etc. – all orbit around our starring role in life. I know it sounds like we're all narcissistic, but am I close to being right?

Louie's message and the one I'm challenging in myself (and you, if you're brave enough to accept the challenge) is simple: can we adjust the camera angle on this 'movie' and instead of being the central character who's 'performing' at center stage, wake up every day with a sense of wonderment about what God is orchestrating and producing in the story we're fortunate enough to be a part of and witness?

Perhaps this is precisely why, when asked in Matthew's gospel account how we should pray, Jesus implores us to start with, *Our Father who art in heaven*, as opposed to starting with our personal petitions. When we're less *self*-focused and more aware of our place in the bigger context of what's transpiring around us, we're more apt to see what God's doing in and through our lives. We're also more likely to recognize who He's placed in our lives intentionally and better able to acknowledge His sovereignty in our journey.

Our lives most-often feel all-important and all-consuming. In reality, from God's perspective, each of us lives a finite number of years in a massive universe that is far beyond our capacity to fathom, much less understand. God is the sovereign Creator of all...we are the created.

It sounds like such a simple paradigm shift but it's difficult because our typical, culturally-influenced view is that the world revolves around us. If we're able to make this mindset transition to being less the 'star' of our world and more a participant in the miraculous things God is up to in our lives, our perspective becomes profoundly different:

- We'll tend to walk with a genuine posture of humility that is centered on serving others, rather than looking to be served. God becomes more and we become less (John 3:30).
- We're far more likely to be authentic and vulnerable because we don't have this false sense that 'the world' and those around us are gazing at us as the star of the show looking to be emulated. It frees us to embrace our true, less-than-perfect self that is deeply loved by God and others all-the-more, regardless of our 'role' in all of this.
- We can't help but have an increased sense of gratitude that we're given the opportunity to be a part of God's bigger story. Knowing confidently that the 'story' ends with an extraordinary, even supernaturally-happy ending for those who follow Jesus. And this gratitude may be the best antidote for the worry that tends to

plague us when we feel as though we have to control every element and every outcome in our lives.

- With confidence that God can be trusted with the outcomes, we're less prone to be negatively impacted by challenging circumstances that occur in our lives.
- We are less inclined to take prideful credit for our successes.
- And finally, instead of feeling the burden to personally solve every problem we encounter, we instead learn to pause long enough to acknowledge God's presence and sovereignty:
  - "Lord, how can I help in this bigger story you are orchestrating?"
  - "How will you use this situation to grow me into the person you've designed me to be?"

Can you fathom the difference in your peace of mind when you stop trying to control every outcome in life? Control is too big a burden for any of us to carry. Instead, challenge yourself to shift your mindset from being the central actor in this thing called "life" and embrace the role of a grateful, awe-struck observer who has the privilege of watching what God is up to every single day. When you do...peace follows.

Let go...

My default mode for too many years had been to take control of any situation and to 'make things happen' in life. Dependence on most anything was uncomfortable. As I'm learning to embrace (and love) this mindset and become far-less 'driven,' my dependence on God and His Spirit working in and through me also becomes more attainable.

I can hear your objections from where I'm writing: It's easy to say, "let go and let God" but it's close to impossible for most of us to put this pithy principle into practice. How does a human, even a Jesus-follower, who is taught from an early age to be independent and self-reliant in life genuinely take his or her hands off the steering wheel of life and let God 'take the wheel'? It's just not our natural inclination!

And yet, when we get this right, it's amazingly liberating because we aren't just relying on our own strength to accomplish whatever we set out to do in life. Instead, we're plugging-in to where God is working and trusting him to equip us to help accomplish His purposes. Paul's words in Philippians are encouraging and reinforce the notion: *I can do all things through Christ who strengthens me* (Phil 4:13).

Best-selling author Sarah Young, in her devotional, *Jesus Calling: Enjoying Peace in His Presence* echoes this encouragement to the reader from Jesus' perspective:

> Follow Me wherever I lead, without worrying about how it will all turn out. Think of your life as an adventure, with Me as your Guide and Companion. Live in the now, concentrating on staying in step with Me.
>
> When our path leads to a cliff, be willing to climb it with My help. When we come to a resting place, take time to be refreshed in My Presence. Enjoy the rhythm of life lived close to Me. You already know the ultimate destination of your journey: your entrance into heaven. So keep your focus on the path just before you, leaving outcomes up to Me.

Try loosening the grip of your hands and invite Jesus to live in and through you. Once you've chosen to embrace the three core *Truths* outlined in the previous section, you'll have the confidence and assurance that God can be trusted with the outcomes.

Do the next, right thing

In case you misinterpreted this first mindset to say, "I don't really have to do anything – just give it all to God" – that's not the message! We still have to be diligent and responsible. We're still on a journey of learning, discovering, and growing so that we're well-equipped to be used by God at work, at home, in church, and in our communities. But we can pursue all of these things with a genuine sense of peace that God can be trusted with the outcomes in our pursuits and in our lives.

And yes, there are times in our lives when we get overwhelmed. We may have more priorities than we can possibly manage; a serious illness that prevents us from doing our work effectively; a semester of difficult courses in college that are challenging and seemingly beyond our capabilities; or perhaps even the pressure of a struggling business or a lingering job search as our bank account dwindles to dangerously low balances.

When there are more alligators in the pond-of-life than you can possibly manage – don't endeavor to accomplish everything at once. This strategy tends to paralyze even the most capable people.

Instead, there's a simple, game-changing principle that's effective amidst overwhelming circumstances: just do the next, right thing! You may be tempted to ruminate on your regrets about how you got into this situation, but you can't change the past. You also can't influence the future much at all, even if you endlessly fret about it. Consider one question that most matters: what's the next, right thing I can do to make progress **today**? And then pause long enough to invite God to give you clarity in identifying your priorities and next steps.

Eventually, as you make progress, you'll pause long enough to poke your head up and realize just how far you've come and how many things you have accomplished – by simply doing the next, right thing. And very often, the best way we can see our progress in the face of difficult circumstances is by looking backwards at where we have come from instead of being daunted by the enormity of what lies ahead. Keep things simple - focus on doing the next right thing and learn to trust God with the rest.

Trust that God will make all things work together for good…so that your peace can prevail

Our faith, confidence and even the strength of our relationship with God is too-often influenced by our current circumstances. When life is good, God is good. When our circumstances are suspect (or worse), we tend to struggle in our faith and feel as though God has somehow abandoned us. You might call it a 'conditional' faith in God.

And yet, Paul's message to us in the Book of Romans assures us that regardless of what happens in our life – nuisances, tragedies, or anything in between – God promises to make lemonade out of life's lemons: *And we know that in all things God works for the good of those who love Him, who have been called according to His purpose* (Rom 8:28).

Our comfort and confidence in embracing this first mindset rests in our knowledge and faith that God can and will bring good from our circumstances. When I understand that God is sovereign, challenges actually become further opportunities to trust God. It doesn't promise that things will turn out exactly as we had planned or envisioned, but it does assure us that God will bring good from it all.

Jesus' words in the last verse of John's gospel reinforce this promise: *"I have told you these things so that in me you may have peace. In this world you will have trouble. But take heart! I have overcome the world!"* (John 16:3).

You've likely recognized that this mindset runs counter to today's cultural messages that bombard us – "You deserve to be happy"; "The answer is in you"; "Where there's a will there's a way" – all of which tend to fuel our sense of self-importance and self-reliance.

And yet, it's this self-reliance and our attempts to maintain control of the outcomes in our lives that leaves us nothing less than exhausted! Left to our own devices, we'll dwell on regrets about our past, obsess about our current circumstances, and endlessly fret about the future...none of which leads to joy or the genuine peace of mind to which most of us aspire. In fact, these tendencies most often create the opposite - inner turmoil. This first mindset frees us to live one-day-at-a-time, trusting that regardless of what happens, we can rest in the promise that God will redeem it all - which is exactly how God created us to live, and thrive!

When we get this right...

We wake up each morning, put our feet (or knees) on the floor and humbly pray, "Lord, I don't know entirely what lies ahead, but I trust you with this day. I'm trusting and grateful that today's activities - my appointments and even the people I meet – are in your care. I'll choose to trust that good will come from whatever may transpire and I pray more than anything, that Your will be done. Help me to see the world as you see it – to celebrate what you celebrate and grieve what breaks your heart. And finally, Lord, I pray that you'll equip me to be a prayerful and peace-filled observer of what you orchestrate and that I have the privilege of witnessing. I will rest well embracing the knowledge that you are sovereign and I am not, thankfully!"

Supporting Scriptures:

- *Many are the plans in a man's heart but the Lord's purpose prevails* (Prov 19:21).
- *Trust in the Lord with all your heart and lean not on your own understanding* (Prov 3:5-6).
- *I am the vine, you are the branches. If you remain in me and I in you, you will bear much fruit; apart from me you can do nothing* (John 15:5).
- *And we know that in all things God works for the good of those who love him and are called according to His purpose* (Rom 8:28).
- *And the peace of God, which transcends all understanding, will guard your hearts and your minds in Christ Jesus* (Phil 4:7).

Mindset # 1: God is in Control

...of the outcomes

Discussion Questions

- Do you generally rely on your own strength and abilities to achieve outcomes in your life or on God?
- Why is it so difficult for us to trust God with the outcomes in our life?
- Are you the central 'actor' in life? What would it take for you to change this perspective?
- What does it mean to *"trust in the Lord with all your heart"* when you're in the midst of challenging circumstances?
- Can you think of adverse circumstances in your past that God has *"worked for good"* in your life? Did you recognize this at the time or subsequently?
- When have you felt most 'peace-filled' in your life? Can you explain how you felt and why?

Recommended Activities

- Make a list of the key expectations and desires in your life currently – about your job, school, children, marriage, finances, etc. Identify which of these expectations/desires are the most difficult to trust God with the outcomes and why?

- Pray that God will equip you to release these expectations (and preoccupations) to Him and give you an extraordinary peace and contentment in doing so.

Mindset #2: Our Calling: Love God and Love Others

...with your skills and your gifts

It's easy to be overwhelmed when you consider God's call on our lives. Particularly if you grew up in a "works-oriented" religious tradition as I did that insists that our relationship with God is somehow contingent on what we do and how we do it. That mindset can put a tremendous and unhealthy burden on any of us.

The other lament I hear often, particularly with job seekers in the C3G career-networking ministry (www.c3g.org) that's been a labor of love for me over many years, sounds something like, "I wish God would my make my calling clearer to me. If I knew what He'd really like me to do, I'd find a way to do it!"

Our calling is simpler than that. Jesus was asked by one of the Pharisees which of the Old Testament laws was most important as a trick question of sorts. His answer was startlingly simple: *'Love the Lord your God with all your heart and with all your soul and with all your mind.' This is the first and greatest commandment. And the second is like it: 'Love your neighbor as yourself'* (Matt 22:37-39).

Consider how liberating this mindset could be if we choose to adopt it. We'd spend a lot less time fretting about doing "enough" or getting more things accomplished. Instead, we'd rest in the confidence that we'll be given plentiful opportunities to love and serve other people as God provides - if we're aware and available enough to be His hands and feet in our journey.

God doesn't keep score based on our worldly successes and accomplishments - although you may very well be successful. He simply calls us to walk each day being aware of the opportunities to love and care about people whose path we cross – at work, school, in the community and even at play.

David Gibson, author of, *Living Life Backwards: How Ecclesiastes teaches us to live in the light of the end,* makes the point that the author of the book of Ecclesiastes, "is deeply committed to a way of being in the world that locates us in a right relationship to God and a right relationship to our neighbor – and from these two things flow all the happiness in life we will ever need for it is there we see ourselves as we truly are: dependent creatures made for relationship with our Creator."

What does it mean to love God?

We have no ability, within ourselves alone, to produce love for God, regardless of how obligated we may feel to do so. We must first receive God's unconditional love and acceptance for us before we will ever learn to love Him in return. Scripture says it simply: *We love because He first loved us* (1 John 4:19). It's the reason our Truth #2 was entirely about accepting the fact that you are deeply and unconditionally loved by God - complete with your successes and failures, and with your incredible strengths and even your embarrassing weaknesses.

Once you accept this truth, the best way to think about loving God in return is the same way you show love to those closest to you. You think about them often. You stay in touch regularly – via the phone, texts, emails, and even face-to-face meetings. You do your best to learn more about them and even to learn *from* them. No relationship can be nurtured and grown without a significant investment of time and energy on your part. Why is it any different with God?

We're also given a significant clue in another verse in Matthew's account of Jesus' Sermon on the Mount: *Seek first the kingdom of God and His righteousness, and all these other things will be provided* (Matt 6:33). We all tend to focus our energy and mindshare on "all these other things" (money, titles, achievements, etc.) that Jesus references in this verse, yet His call is provocatively different, and profoundly simple: seek Him first!

Even the biblical account of Martha and Mary gives us a profound hint about our call to love and worship God when Martha was frustrated that her sister Mary was worshipping at the feet of Jesus instead of helping with the chores. "Martha, Martha," the Lord answered, "you are worried and upset about many things, but few things are needed—or indeed only one. Mary has chosen what is better, and it will not be taken away from her." (Luke 10:42-43).

What about you - If you were in a court of law and on trial to determine if you are 'guilty' of loving God...would you be 'convicted'? God wants your trial to be an open and shut case and conclusion – guilty as charged...of loving God deeply!

...and what about loving others?

The most tangible way we can love God is by loving the people that God gives us the privilege of being with – in any and all settings. We're called to be his hands and feet here on earth. Filled with the Holy Spirit, we're even called to allow God's love to flow in and through us: *for it is God who works in you to will and to act in order to fulfill his good purpose* (Phil 2:13).

The Greek word for the type of love we're called to share is 'agape' love, which doesn't depend on our feelings. It literally means the conscious act of loving someone else in your orbit, regardless of their response. It's this kind of love that may be the most powerful way for any of us to share the good news that Jesus exemplified – that those we meet are deeply loved by God. And the way they'll experience God's love is through our small and significant acts of love and kindness.

Author Bob Goff consistently implores us in his books and videos not to overcomplicate this calling 'thing': just love people – *everywhere, always!* This love can come in the form of financial generosity or something potentially more transformational like the blessing of your time or your personal giftedness.

Jesus used the metaphor of the vine and the branches in John's gospel to explain that loving others well doesn't require your own strength or brilliance. Instead, you and I are the branch attached to the fruit-bearing vine that is God's love (John 15). We're simply called to be willing and available to allow Jesus to work in and through us to love others well.

It's not about being more committed either – commitment is what I am promising to do for God. It's far more like surrender - placing my life in His hands to do as He purposes.

Judging others

One thing that impedes our ability to love others is our tendency to judge others. Have you considered how frequently you judge other people? Your immediate reaction is likely, "Almost never!"

I've become more aware of this convicting habit lately and I'm embarrassed to admit that I am guilty as charged. I'm also suspicious that I'm not alone. Here are some not so proud examples of scenarios and the corresponding small, but nevertheless judgmental, voice in my head:

- Sitting across the restaurant from a couple that are completely distracted by their respective smart phones and not talking to each other – "I can't believe they would make that choice."

- Getting seated next to an overweight man in the coach section of an airplane – "It isn't fair that I have my comfort compromised by someone else's size on a four-hour flight in confined quarters."
- Or, a young mother in a coffee shop seated near you has two loud, disruptive children that are negatively impacting your ability to be productive – "She should do a better job of disciplining her children!"

I know those are pedestrian examples but they highlight how many times in any given day that we're tempted to, or worse yet, do judge people. Conduct your own experiment today and catch yourself in these temptations to be critical - you might be surprised to find that you're more judgmental than you think.

Carey Nieuwhof is a leadership author and podcaster who recently posted an article entitled, *The three things Christian do that non-Christians despise*. The first on the list is about our tendency to judge others and here's his excerpt:

> It doesn't take long for non-Christians to tell you how much they hate the way Christians judge other people. Two minutes on social media will reveal Christians and preachers condemning unchurched people for their sexual habits and preferences, life-style choices and even political views. I doubt this is what Jesus had in mind when he gave his life in love for the world.

> Disclosure: without the mercy and intervention of Christ, I'm very judgmental. And years ago, I realized how devastating judgment and criticism can be to others. So...I'm waging a life-long battle against it. Confessing it, repenting of it almost daily. I realized years ago that very few people get judged into life

change. Far more get loved into it. It also occurred to me that the presence of judgment almost always guarantees an absence of love.

Think about it through the lens of your marriage, a friendship or even someone you work with: it is virtually impossible to love someone and judge someone at the same time. But wait, you ask: what if they're making a mistake and I need to correct them? First of all, look at your mistakes and the depth of your sin, and deal with your issues first. In the process, you'll encounter a loving God who forgives you despite your rather egregious sin. And having been loved, you can love others.

I try to remember this rule: If I'm judging someone, I'm not loving them. You can't judge someone and love them at the same time. What would happen if Christians stopped judging the world (isn't that God's job?) and started loving it instead? I believe that's what Jesus did.

The Bible is remarkably clear about our temptation to judge:

- Jesus said to the crowd who were intent to stone the woman caught in adultery, *"He that is without sin among you, let him first cast a stone at her"* (John 8:7).
- In another part of the Gospels, Jesus is quoted as saying, *"For in the same way you judge others, you will be judged, and with the measure you use, it will be measured to you"* (Matt 7:2).

Knowing that judging is our innate tendency, often to help to make ourselves feel better about our own hang-ups and dysfunctions, what if we gave up judging others entirely and instead focused all of our time and energy on loving those we're fortunate to be with each day?

Work (and love) as though working for the Lord

How do we 'operationalize' this notion of loving God and loving others where we spend the vast majority of our time and energy – in our vocations and avocations? In Paul's words: *Whatever you do, work at it with all your heart, as working for the Lord, not for man* (Col 3:23).

Let's break this verse into its three parts:
- *Whatever you do* – What does that include? Job search? Your small (or large) business? Does that include being a stay-at-home parent? Being a volunteer? The answer: it captures all of the above!
- *Work at it with all your heart* – What does this really mean? It's clearly not 'do the minimum required to accomplish the task'. Instead, it seems far more about pursuing your work and your priorities in an excellent way and with every gift God gave you – including your time, your skills and your God-given resources.
- *...as working for the Lord, not for man*! How much different would your daily tasks and responsibilities feel if you dedicated all of your time and effort to God? How much more purposeful would you feel if you knew your efforts were glorifying to God above all? Embracing this paradigm becomes a testament to your joy, to your attitude of excellence; and to your commitment to serving others. Your vocational calling is truly "sacred" – not just "secular."

When you do this well, those closest to you who observe your countenance can't help but ponder, "I don't know what it is about Beth, but there's something different, and special about the way she operates each day – and I want some of what she has." Living a life that exemplifies Jesus may be the most profound calling of all – sharing *the reason for your hope* with your actions, not just your words (1 Pet 3:15).

To those who are given much, much is expected

You may read this second mindset and struggle with negative 'self-talk': "Yea, but I don't have many skills that allow me to fulfill this calling to love others..." or, "I don't have the time or the resources that others have to do this well."

Let's approach these objections from two perspectives. First, we're all gifted in our own, unique ways. Just because you're an introvert, doesn't mean God can't use your giftedness in powerful ways. Just because you don't have a college degree or make less money than others you know, doesn't mean you can't profoundly love someone in your life today.

Loving others doesn't require a heroic act – and most often it isn't! For more often it's small acts of kindness and care - a smile, offering to help someone, or a word of encouragement – that will most profoundly impact the greatest number of people in your circle of influence.

The second perspective is addressed in Luke's gospel when he captures the moment that Jesus challenges all of us to use our unique giftedness: *To the one who is given much, much will be expected* (Luke 12:48). In the same way that we're not equally gifted, we're also not expected to love others in identical ways. God knows exactly how he designed you and He did it brilliantly and intentionally – with your personal giftedness, skills, and even your weaknesses. He's simply calling us to use whatever we've been given for the benefit of others – all to His glory.

There are two significant impediments to embracing mindset #2. First, it's the nagging sense that we always have to do more - more Bible studies, more quiet time, more scripture memory verses, or anything else you can name (and have likely tried). It can be nothing short of exhausting.

And the other is the angst we tend to feel because we don't have clarity on what, specifically, God is calling us to do. And it's this struggle that I've spent much of the last 20 years studying, praying about, and walking with countless Christian job seekers who share this struggle. But the struggle is misplaced - because our ultimate calling is far simpler than most think. You and I are called to love God and to manifest that love as a light in the world by loving those around you. It's really that simple.

God has called us to cast our burdens and our anxiety on Him, and he promises to give us rest. Do you recognize how life-giving this second mindset could be compared to the pressure we often put on ourselves to achieve and succeed – for no apparent eternal purpose? What mindset will you choose?

When we get this right...

We recognize that God simply wants us to be His. He wants all of us - a deep, intimate relationship with Him and with those that He puts in our lives. He has gifted you purposefully and He will equip you to love and serve others well – if you're willing and available. By doing so you'll demonstrate your love and commitment to Him and experience the joy, peace, and purposefulness that is so elusive when we have a mindset primarily focused on achieving earthly pursuits that matter so little in God's realm.

"Lord Jesus, may I recognize the opportunities you give me today to use the gifts and talents you've blessed me with in a way that shares Your love with others. Please help me to resist my innate temptation to judge which will compromise my ability to love them well. May I walk this journey faithfully and with all of my heart – for your glory."

Supporting Scriptures:

- *Seek first the kingdom of God and His righteousness, and all these other things will be provided* (Matt 6:33).
- *For in the same way you judge others, you will be judged, and with the measure you use, it will be measured to you* (Matt 7:2).
- *Whatever you do, work at it with all your heart, as working for the Lord, not for man* (Col 3:23)
- *To he who is given much, much will be expected* (Luke 12:48).

Mindset #2: Our Calling: Love God and Love Others
...with your skills and your gifts

Discussion Questions

- If a close friend asked you about God's calling on your life – what would you tell them?
- What does it really mean to you to *love God with all your heart and with all your soul and with all your mind?*
- What prevents us from making 'loving God and loving others' the priority it should be?
- What are the skills and gifts that God has equipped you with for the benefit of others? Do you feel as though you're using these skills in a way that God designed? Why or why not?
- Can you think of examples when judging people has compromised your ability to love them well?
- What role does the Holy Spirit play in equipping us to love God and love others?
- How difficult is it to, *"work as though working for the Lord"* when you're doing tasks that are unfulfilling?

Recommended Activities

- Find some time to quietly journal to identify the ways that you love God and love others. Ask the Holy Spirit to reveal some small (and perhaps profound) ways that you can love even more.
- Identify the tasks and responsibilities you perform that tend to be least fulfilling or most menial – and ask God to equip you with the ability to choose a healthy mindset that allows these tasks to become "worship" – *as though working for the Lord!*

Mindset #3: Becoming Christ-like

...is a journey

"None of us really fall in love, we just stop making everything about ourselves, and love floods into the space selfishness leaves behind"

Bob Goff

For the follower of Jesus, your life is a journey each day to grow in Christ-likeness. It's the process of becoming who Jesus would be if he were you.

I've wrestled with God on plenty of issues but the most consistent topic has been about our ultimate purpose here on earth: why did you create me and what have you called me to do or accomplish? I'm certainly not alone in this struggle. Mindset #3 is focused on helping to answer these questions.

Before we get there, let's keep in mind Truth #3 that we've already covered: Jesus, first and foremost, invites us to <u>choose</u> to follow Him by making the decision to accept His gift of salvation that His death and resurrection offers.

Once we make this choice, and because we're then blessed and equipped with the gift of His Holy Spirit, we're then on a journey to grow to be more and more like Jesus for the balance of our life here on planet Earth. Some call this sanctification; others might refer to it as holiness. The simplest way for me to understand this calling: it's all about becoming more and more Christ-like.

These first three mindsets were captured well by Major Ian Thomas many years ago in what he called the "threefold interlock" – A life of faith is our love **for** God (Mindset #2), resulting in our dependency **upon** God (Mindset #1), resulting in our obedience **to** God (Mindset #3).

If you've never studied the Biblical support for our call to Christ-likeness, it's distinct (emphasis is mine):

- *"Whoever says he abides in Him ought to walk in the same way in which He* (Jesus) *walked"* (1 John 2:6).
- *For this is the will of God, your sanctification* (meaning: to be used for its original purpose – our holiness) (1Thes 4:3).
- *For those God foreknew he also predestined to be conformed to the image of His son...* (Rom 8:29).

Who wouldn't want to become more Christ-like? Doing so allows us to grow closer to God, it means He is in greater control of our lives, and it ultimately brings glory to Him in the process. It literally brings to life the concept of Christ living in and through us and allows us to experience the 'fruit' that we're promised as He increases and we decrease: *love, joy, peace, forbearance, kindness, goodness, faithfulness, gentleness and self-control* (Gal 2:20, 5:22-23). Did you notice that the first three of this 'fruit' are precisely what most of us find elusive – *love, joy,* and *peace*? This is why Christ-likeness matters so much!

And yet, it's easier said than done.

What is Christ-like, really?

Let's make this practical and go straight to the source – Jesus Himself. Read through the four gospel accounts that chronicle the three years of Jesus' adult ministry and see if you can capture the essence of his attributes. I'm guessing you'll conclude there are some consistent themes:

- His identity was not about impressing others but entirely centered on His relationship with God, the Father, where his peace and purpose were derived.
- He loved purely, not conditionally - and even loved those who betrayed him.
- He taught us that life and love isn't fair or equitable - consider the parable of the talents whose laborers worked in the fields for equal pay with entirely unequal workloads.
- He was the model of patience – even if someone didn't know nearly as much as He did.
- He was the epitome of grace-filled – providing unmerited favor to Peter, Lazarus, and even the thief beside Him on the cross at Calvary.
- He didn't waiver from speaking truth, and yet was quick to forgive – remember the woman at the well who lived an immoral lifestyle?
- He genuinely believed in the capabilities of others, especially when we abide in Him– saying to Peter when he walked on the water, *"take courage"* and *"come to me."*
- He was obedient and strong when facing temptation – especially with Satan in the desert.
- He was entirely self-less – literally sacrificing his own life.
- He was filled with the Holy Spirit and perfectly in-step with His heavenly Father – an audience of one.
- He was content in his circumstances – even if they were far-less-than-stellar circumstances.

- And yet, he was fully human like us – walked as we do, talked as we do, needed rest as we do, and challenged as we are!

This list strikes me as a seemingly unattainably high bar for the rest of us, especially in our own strength. I, for one, have a long way to go. What about you? Perhaps the list of attributes above can be translated into one simple summary of what becoming Christ-like is all about: it's the process of transforming us from being naturally and innately selfish to being genuinely concerned about the well-being of others.

This is the life-long journey we're on. And it's most-often your trials and tribulations, and a few key relationships, that God will use to help you grow into the Christ-like person He designed you to be.

Trials and challenges accelerate our Christ-like journey

"Hardship often prepares an ordinary person for an extraordinary destiny" – C.S. Lewis

A good friend of mine and a retired Pastor from Northpoint Community Church, John Woodall, is an amazing encourager of men and regularly suggests that we'd all be wise to develop a retrospective 'life map' that visually captures our life's journey. To be useful, it should include our most significant life events (both 'highs' and 'lows') and our corresponding spiritual walk with God. It visually makes obvious how God uses both our successes and especially our trials to make us into the people He designed us to be.

Joni Eareckson Tada may be the poster-person for growing and thriving in spite of significant setbacks and challenges. Now in her 60's, she was paralyzed in a diving accident when she was a teenager. She's experienced chronic pain since the accident and has long-been confined to a wheelchair. And yet, her reputation for exuding a positive attitude is inspiring. An interviewer once asked her, "Joni, how do you manage to be so radiant in the midst of your pain and suffering?" Her response, "Jim, every day I find reasons amid my pain to be thankful for life...I guess that has become my reflex reaction for my life." Sounds like a glimpse of Christ-likeness...

Or let's use an example you may have experienced at one time or another: losing your job. Having walked with many job seekers in the past 2 decades I can attest that a job loss is very difficult for most. It shakes our confidence; challenges our finances; and creates stress like few other life-events. And yet, it's also become very obvious to me that God uses job transitions to profoundly re-arrange our priorities, change our paradigms, and to draw us closer to Him in the process – if we allow Him to do so.

We've already established that God loves you exactly as you are (Mindset #2) – and yet this third mindset suggests that He loves you too much to leave you that way. The apostle Paul captures this concept well, *I consider that our present sufferings are not worth comparing with the glory that will be revealed in us* (Rom 8:18).

Jesus' brother, James reinforces this point: *Count it all joy, my brothers, when you meet trials of various kinds, for you know that the testing of your faith produces steadfastness. And let steadfastness have its full effect, that you may be perfect and complete, lacking in nothing* (Jas 1:2-4).

Instead of looking at adverse circumstances as daunting, adopt the mindset that while they will be challenging, these adversities are serving an important purpose in God's design - to make us more Christ-like! When we embrace this purpose, we can make the choice to thank God for the trials that we face – whether small or significant.

Marriage: God's strategic relationship to make us more Christ-like

I won't pretend to know all of God's strategic designs for different institutions and relationships when He created our world and each of us occupants. However, some are more obvious than others – like His purpose for the Church. We, the Church, are the community designed by God for His followers to love, care for, and ultimately build each other up while also sharing the good news of our faith in Jesus with the broader community of those that don't yet believe.

When it comes to marriage though, God's purpose always seemed practically simple to me: to create a unique relationship between a man and woman that fosters procreation; provides the parental leadership in a family structure that enables children to thrive and ultimately become functioning adults; and of course, the utilitarian purpose that two are better than one and we naturally complement each other in our strengths, skills, etc. What else could there possibly be to a marriage relationship?

It turns out, plenty...and here's a warning label for readers: understanding the answer to this provocative question will profoundly impact you, your marriage, and your path to Christ-likeness.

Let's approach this from the husband's perspective for a moment. If God's ultimate desire for husbands is to sanctify us and to make us more Christ-like in our time here on earth, it's perfectly logical that He would use the vulnerable, relentlessly-transparent marriage relationship as a primary mechanism to help us in this journey. In fact. He's using your spouse as a full-length mirror to 'reflect' how you're doing as a husband in your path to Christ-likeness.

When we understand and embrace this concept, it changes everything about your marriage and its purpose. It becomes less about the utilitarian and practical purposes outlined above, and far more about the spiritual purpose that God designed into our marriages.

If you're anything like me, it's relatively easy to be perceived as patient, kind, loving, and peace-filled by friends and acquaintances who see you in environments when you're on your best behavior. But Devonie, my wife of more than 40 years now, knows the whole truth and nothing but the truth. If I want clarity (and often demoralizing clarity) on how I'm doing in becoming more self-less and loving, the most accurate 'full-length mirror' for me is Devonie.

It's this vulnerable 'nakedness' between spouses that makes marriage so sacred in God's design. God desires us to grow in Christ-likeness and marriage is the single most important institution He designed for this purpose for those who are married. Pause on that thought a moment. In all the years we're fortunate enough to live here on Earth, God has purposed your marriage as a primary vehicle to draw us closer to Him by giving us clarity on how we're doing in becoming more Christ-like...if we let Him.

While this book is focused on a short list of broader 'life' mindsets, my work with marriages has taught me that there's an equally important set of mindsets related to marriage relationships. When husbands and wives embrace these, they have the potential to transform even a struggling marriage. Here are a few brief, yet illustrative examples:

- **Assume the best of intentions in your spouse, not the worst**. It's easy (and common) to 'read between the lines' of your spouses' comments or questions and assume they were intent on hurting you. Doing so is both detrimental and often an inaccurate assumption. Instead, choose to assume that your spouse's question or comment had the best of intentions.
- **Decide to be happily incompatible.** – Most spouses are more dissimilar than they are similar. We can either be annoyed by these differences or we can consciously

decide that my proclivities are different but not necessarily better than those of my spouse. In essence, <u>choose</u> and commit to being happily incompatible with your spouse.

- **Divorce is not an option.** If a couple keeps divorce as their plan "B" (in case things don't work out in their marriage), they're going to find that things are far less likely to work out because it becomes a self-fulfilling prophecy. <u>Choose</u> a marriage covenant where divorce is not an option.
- **Love is a verb, not a feeling.** This mindset won't be crucial in the first 6 months of your marriage, but after the infatuation subsides, you'll both need to <u>choose</u> to love each other regardless of how you may "feel." It's this unconditional love that allows marriages to survive and thrive "until death do us part."
- **Forgive...sooner than later.** Which we'll cover in more detail in Mindset #6 of this book.

The marriage that adopts these marital mindsets will experience far more joy and peace in their marriage, but also in their lives. And their children may be the biggest beneficiaries of all.

You can get far more details on these principles and related resources at my website: <u>www.menyourmarriagematters.com</u>

We are called to Christ-likeness and every challenge, every relationship, and every circumstance in our lives can be used by God (if we allow Him to do so) to make us more like his Son, Jesus. And when adverse circumstances arise, instead of becoming discouraged, resolve to pause for a moment and ask instead, "Lord, how will You use this circumstance to grow my Christ-likeness on the path to becoming the person you designed me to be?" The opportunity for each of us rests in our ability to adopt a Christ-like mindset that is contrary to our innately selfish and prideful ways.

When we get this right...

Embracing Mindset #3 is an upside down, counter-cultural choice. "Lord, help me to understand and embrace the mind and spirit of your son Jesus – to love as he loved; to sacrifice as He sacrificed; and to pray and stay connected in a personal relationship with you, continuously. Open my eyes and my heart to all that you are accomplishing through my difficulties.

And in this way, help me to rest in the knowledge that you'll grow and equip me to be used as a light in an otherwise dark and broken world."

Supporting Scriptures:

- *Whoever claims to live in Him must live as Jesus lived* (1 John 2:6).
- *For this is the will of God, your sanctification...* (1 Thes 4:3).
- *For those God foreknew he also predestined to be conformed to the image of His son* (Rom 8:29).
- *But the fruit of the Spirit is love, joy, peace, forbearance, kindness, goodness, faithfulness, gentleness and self-control....* (Gal 5: 22-23).
- *I have told you these things, so that in me you may have peace. In this world you will have trouble. But take heart! I have overcome the world* (John 16:33).
- *Husbands, love your wives, just as Christ loved the church and gave himself up for her* (Eph 5:25).

Mindset #3: Becoming Christ-like

...is a journey

Discussion Questions

- What does it really mean to be more "Christ-like" in your words?
- What most prevents us from being more Christ-like?
- Are we each born innately selfish or is it a learned behavior? Explain your perspective...
- Why do trials and challenges in our lives help us to grow in Christ-likeness? Can you provide examples in your own life?
- For those who are married: why is marriage so strategic in our path to becoming more Christ-like?

Recommended Activities

- Find at least 5 verses in scripture that make it clear that being "Christ-like" is God's call for the Jesus-follower.
- Self-examination: How would an objective, 'full-length-mirror' assess your progress in the journey to Christ-likeness? Can we be a good judge of our own progress?
- Pray that God will increasingly give you the heart, the mind, and the spirit of Jesus – and use you as the *branch*, connected to His *vine* in loving and serving others.

Mindset #4: Choose Not to Worry!

...it's an imperative, not a suggestion

It's beyond dispute, life will present us with countless challenges and preoccupations. There are plenty of things for us to fret about – including regrets about the past (which we can do nothing to change) and worries about the future (most of which is a waste of energy).

God is crystal clear in the Bible that worry is not in His design for us:

- ..._do_ _not_ _worry_ _about your life, what you will eat or drink..._ (Matt 6:25).
- _Do_ _not_ _be_ _anxious_ _about_ _anything_... (Phil 4:6). (Note: more evidence that worry is a pervasive issue for most: Phil 4:6-7 is the single, most highlighted Bible passage on the Amazon Kindle platform as of 2019)

It sounds declarative and definitive...and yet, we're prone to excessive worry.

As Arthur Brooks, author and self-professed expert on happiness contends, "If you have no control over an event, no amount of rumination can help you. It can only lower your happiness further."

One could argue that a modicum of worry is actually healthy. I've even argued that position, "It's called _planning_." While thinking about what's ahead and planning accordingly is useful, ruminating endlessly about the array of potential negative outcomes in a situation provides almost no value...but we continue to worry.

We worry about our children – will they learn enough? Will they have good friends? Will they get into the college they've chosen? Will they marry the right person?

We worry about our finances – will we have enough? Will we ever retire? Will I get a sufficient pay raise?

We even worry about what others think of us – will they like me? Did I say the wrong thing? Is my credibility shot? Will I ever see them again...and do I even want to? Left to our own devices, we have the propensity to worry about virtually everything.

[Note: Before we explore this topic further, there are people who are diagnosed with clinical anxiety. That is not the focus of this discussion and mental health professionals are increasingly well-equipped to help manage this type of anxiety. Mental illness is as 'real' a health ailment as any physiological ailment and deserves the appropriate treatment and therapy.]

For most, worry is really the gentle word for fear: fear of what's ahead; fear of the unknown; or even fear of failure.

I still remember a former mentor of mine challenging me, in a helpful way, about a career change I was considering many years ago when he sensed that I was fearful about making the change. Specifically, I was worried that I may not be successful in the new role. He challenged me with this question: "Do you know what your 'fear' is Peter?" I had my own guess but I wasn't courageous enough to offer an answer. So, I asked, "No, Dan, what is fear?" His answer was convicting: "Fear is really just a lack of faith."

Dan was right – when we obsessively worry and that worry transforms to fear, we're adopting an unhealthy mindset that God can't really be trusted with this situation. And our common response to this lack of faith is to worry some more. It's a vicious cycle.

How do we embrace a new, healthier mindset that equips us to stop the cycle of worry and yet still deal with the speed bumps that are inevitable in life? And since we know that we're going to experience challenges and setbacks, how do we best manage them without being consumed by worry? Three simple principles may help you embrace Mindset #4 and they demonstrate the inter-relationships between all of these mindsets:

- God doesn't give us challenges beyond what we can handle (1 Cor 10:13). I've always taken great comfort in the way retired Pastor and Author Tim Keller explains this perspective: "If you knew everything that God knows, you'd give yourself exactly what He's given you."
- When trials do confront us, harken back to Mindset #3 (our journey to Christ-likeness) – these trials will be used by God to help you grow in Christ-likeness. When you adopt this paradigm, you'll no longer look at challenging circumstances with disdain but with confidence that God will use these adverse situations for your good and for your growth (Rom 8:28).
- And, as we outlined in Mindset #1 (God's in control), when we truly embrace the mindset that we can trust God with the outcomes in our lives – it enables us to consciously stop fretting about what the future may hold and instead, peacefully anticipate what may come.

It bears repeating – worrying (or not) is a choice we each make, often sub-consciously. We have to fight our innate and somewhat natural tendency to worry as a default – but it **is** our conscious choice to make.

The antidotes to worry

If worry is unhelpful, what's the solution? If you spend too much time and energy thinking (and worrying) about what lies ahead, here are a few suggestions that have proven helpful as I've personally waged this anti-worry 'battle' - each of which we'll expand on in more depth below:

- **Stay present and in the moment** – in our tasks, in our relationships, and even in our rest. Every mental cycle we spend on the future, or on things beyond our control, is a significant moment not spent enjoying or appreciating what you're doing right now.
- **Don't worry about tomorrow…put it on the calendar** – a significant contributor to our worry is related to the way we manage our time and our calendar and it's 'fixable'!
- **Manage your expectations and embrace contentment** – contentment is being satisfied, or even delighted with what we have today, not preoccupied with what we long to have. And our expectations will profoundly impact our contentment and our inclination to worry.
- **Resist a sense of entitlement** – fight the tendency to believe that life should be 'fair' because inevitably it's not fair and then we're prone to disappointment, or even bitterness. The choice to resist feeling entitled is also ours to make.
- **Cultivate gratefulness** – when our focus is on the future, we compromise our ability to be grateful for exactly what we have today – the people we're surrounded by, the job that we're fortunate enough to occupy, or even the resources God has provided.

- **Pray without ceasing** – Paul implores us to pray "continuously" – which sounds like A LOT! Prayer is a momentary acknowledgement that God is integral to every aspect of our life. And it's these acknowledgments that help loosen worry's unyielding grip on us.

Stay present and in the moment

How much of your mental capacity do you spend thinking about the future? In fact, not just thinking about it but worrying, planning or generally being pre-occupied about tomorrow, next week, or even next year?

I tend to be planning-oriented and a few people close to me contend that one of my strengths is the ability to anticipate what's ahead and then prepare well for what is to come. On one hand, it sounds like a great asset. On the other hand, I'm increasingly convicted that there's a limit to how proactive and planning-oriented we're designed to be. Taken to an extreme, this "strength" translates to excessive worry, obsession and even an exaggerated sense that we can control our own futures and outcomes (reference Mindset #1).

The one thing we're assured of in our lives is the moment and the place that we reside in right now...today. How many times do we hear about a friend, or an acquaintance that has recently died and our first lament is usually, "Life is too short!" And yet, isn't it true that most of us immediately revert back to our natural tendency to spend an inordinate amount of time planning and fretting about what's to come instead of living richly in the present moment?

Let's borrow a concept from Stephen Covey's best-selling book, *The 7 Habits of Highly Effective People* that he calls the 'Circle of Influence.' Covey argued that we spend too much time, energy and mind-share on things we can't directly impact – what he calls the circle of concern (see graphic below).

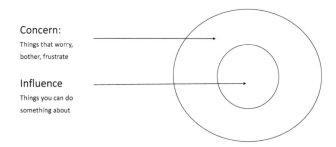

Concern:
Things that worry,
bother, frustrate

Influence
Things you can do
something about

Doing so causes us to worry about things with almost no return on invested time or energy. Instead, if we spend our waking hours focused on the things we can influence and control (our behavior as a simple example), we'll be far more productive and waste less time on things beyond our control.

A few years back I would spend far too many cycles pre-occupied by national politics (which can be downright depressing by the way). Even though my ability to impact our nation's politics is infinitesimal at best, I wasted precious (and finite) brain cycles on things I couldn't really impact. What's changed in the last few years? I still try to stay abreast of major developments and I certainly vote when and where I have the opportunity, but I now spend very little time and almost no energy focused on national politics. Nor do I let it impact my joy anymore. Mine was a conscious choice to stop worrying about it – almost cold turkey.

The scriptures couldn't be clearer (or more consistent) that we're designed in this way:

Yet you do not know what tomorrow will bring. What is your life? For you are a mist that appears for a little time and then vanishes (Jas 4:14).

Therefore do not be anxious about tomorrow, for tomorrow will be anxious for itself. Sufficient for the day is its own trouble (Matt 6:34).

Do not boast about tomorrow, for you do not know what a day may bring (Prov 27:1).

Sarah Young's devotional book, *Jesus Calling* captures this concept brilliantly as she writes from God's perspective to her readers:

> Stop trying to work things out before their times have come. Accept the limitations of living one day at a time. When something comes to your attention, ask Me (God) whether or not it is part of today's agenda. If it isn't, release it into My care and go about today's duties. When you follow this practice, there will be a beautiful simplicity about your life: *a time for everything, and everything in its time* (Ecc 3:1). A life lived close to Me is not complicated or cluttered.

It's a liberating and life-giving perspective!

Don't worry about tomorrow...put it on the calendar!

The objection I hear most often to this principle is, "I get it – I should live in the present; but I've got an abundance of 'to do's' to get 'to done'. How do I balance this relentless tension?"

First, let's put things in context. Why would God create humans as the only species blessed with a mind that is capable of even pondering (or fretting) about the future, and then have the scripture implore us not to obsess about our future?

This tension can be managed - living fully in the present day, planning effectively for the future, and yet not being weighed down excessively by fears and worries about either the past or the future. The answer lies in a few, simple time-management principles that I've been teaching for 20+ years:

1) It starts with identifying your priorities that really matter – personally and professionally. Stop and consider: what really matters in your life that isn't getting the focus and attention that it deserves? Spending more time with your 10-year-old son? More quiet time to better-manage your work/life balance? Learning a new skill? Strengthening your marriage? Completing a new project at work? What does this list look like for you? (BTW - far too many people don't have enough clarity about the answer to this all-important question.)

2) Next, determine what tasks and activities will help you achieve these priorities. Priorities only get accomplished if you identify the tasks or prerequisites necessary to accomplish them.

3) And finally, proactively designate calendar time (i.e., "appointments") for these tasks/activities that allow you to accomplish what really matters. These tasks can be scheduled over the course of days, weeks or even months, depending on the nature of the tasks and your sense of urgency. The principle is simple – putting them on the calendar will ensure you allocate the time and mental energy to actually get them accomplished. Not doing so will result in your time being dominated by less important (and less purposeful) tasks.

When I'm diligent in sticking to the principles outlined above, it results in a calm and peace in my day (and life) that is hard to describe and elusive to most. I can wake up on any given day, look at my calendar for that day with clarity about the key appointments and priority tasks that I've previously aimed to accomplish that day, and know that the day will be purpose-filled. The bonus advantage is I don't feel any pressure (or worries) about priorities or tasks that loom in the future because all of those are captured on the calendar on a subsequent day that is allocated for those tasks.

When you choose to embrace these simple disciplines, the value is significant:

- It will ensure you are focused on the right priorities
- You won't dread (or feel overwhelmed) each day because your calendar only includes tasks that can be reasonably accomplished that day
- And, you'll sleep better at night – because you don't feel "behind." You're actually "ahead" because there is a time and a place on your calendar in the future for everything that really matters.

Manage your expectations and embrace contentment

Much of our worry and mindshare can also be focused on our aspirations and expectations for the future. You may argue, "How can that possibly be bad?" Maybe it's our desire to move to a new, bigger house. Is it a career change you've always wanted to make? Or a dream vacation that's been on your bucket list forever? Those desires and aspirations aren't innately bad...until they morph into your expectations. Therein lies the challenge – because our expectations often lead to profound disappointments when they aren't met.

Think about this concept – there are only two ways to close the expectation/reality gap: you can substantially improve your current reality (not always easy to do) or you can let go of some expectations. Said another way - the less we expect, the happier we'll be!

You may bristle at the notion of giving up a dream by lowering your expectations. But you don't have to give up the dream! You do, though, have the ability (and the choice) to manage your expectations for the sake of your own happiness.

Such a simple concept can be stunningly powerful. It makes me recall a short fable that highlights this point. I've tried to find the author but to no avail – see if this strikes you as it did me:

> *An American businessman struck up a conversation with a fisherman in a small coastal Mexican village. Noticing his fairly small catch, the American asked why he didn't stay out longer and try for a bigger catch. The fisherman said he had enough to support his family's immediate needs.*
>
> *"What do you do with the rest of your time?" the American asked.*
>
> *"I sleep late, fish a little, play with my children, take a siesta with my wife, Maria, stroll into the village each evening where I sip wine and play guitar with my amigos. I have a full and busy life, señor."*
>
> *"I am a Harvard MBA and could help you," said the scoffing American, who proceeded to advise him to buy a bigger boat and eventually a whole fleet, followed by a cannery, and then have enough money to move to a big city to run his expanding business empire.*
>
> *"What then, señor?"*
>
> *The American told him he'd be a millionaire.*
>
> *"Then what, señor?"*

"Then you would retire and move to a small coastal fishing village where you would sleep late, fish a little, play with your kids, take a siesta with your wife, stroll to the village in the evenings where you could sip wine and play your guitar with your amigos."

The irony: we spend so much time chasing "the dream" only to find, often too late in our lives, that what we really treasure is often what we already have. That's what contentment is about in practical terms – loving what you have instead of wanting what you don't have.

Paul wrote about this principle, *...for I have learned to be content whatever the circumstances. I know what it is to be in need and I know what it is to have plenty. I have learned the secret of being content in any and every situation, whether well fed or hungry, whether living in plenty or in want. I can do everything through him who gives me strength* (Phil 4:11-13).

What about you? Do you have a happiness 'gap'? Have you considered letting go of some of your expectations in order to love what you have instead of wanting something more?

Resist a sense of entitlement

Another factor that profoundly impacts our tendency to worry and ultimately our happiness, or lack thereof, is an unhealthy sense of entitlement.

What does entitlement sound like? "Why did this have to happen to me?" "I deserve better!" Or, "I can't believe God let this happen!"

Indeed, life can be tragic and often not "fair." But the premise of these statements assumes that each of us is entitled to a healthy, happy, and mostly-trouble-free existence. Anything that occurs that compromises that expectation is viewed by us as being unfair.

Which begs the question, what *is* fair in life? Are we entitled to a perfect path or should our expectations be adjusted to anticipate and even expect trials?

When I was 9 years old and there were 7 children in our family (ranging in age from 13 to 1 year old), my mother died unexpectedly of complications related to Colitis. Admittedly, I didn't really understand what it meant to grieve that tragic loss well but as I reflect back on that event and the subsequent years of my life, there are two distinct ways I could have processed that loss:

1. I could have clung to the notion that I deserved to have my mother for at least my entire childhood (or more) and anything less than that was entirely unfair and cruel. Embracing this perspective would have likely created a bitterness that would have permeated my entire outlook on life. Or...
2. For whatever reason, I had a different mindset – that I had the gift of my loving mother for 9 years and the blessing of a loving Father and family ever since. Their love has been more than I could have hoped for or fathomed.

Do you see the contrast and the choice? There's a great advantage in resisting the sense that you've been victimized when something adverse happens in your life. Instead, we each have the choice and the capacity to accept the reality that 'stuff' we don't like or expect happens. And when it does, it actually strengthens and equips us to adapt to adverse circumstances more effectively in the future. We also grow as a result – by becoming more Christ-like and avoiding a lingering disappointment or bitterness.

This can only happen when our expectation is that we're not really 'entitled' to anything at all. It bears repeating - God doesn't <u>cause</u> bad things to happen to us but when they do occur, *He (God) can make all things work together for good* – even the things that are painful for us or those we love (Rom 8:28).

Cultivate gratefulness

This one sounds simple but our propensity to worry gets in our way. Here's the 'habit' I'd recommend: wake up each morning and resolve to adopt a deep sense of gratitude for the gifts in your life...for your job; for special relationships; for your family; and for any and all resources that God has graciously provided.

The 'homework' exercise I've often challenged job seekers to do when they're spending too much time worrying and not enough time being grateful is simple. Take a pad of lined paper and a pen and write down everything in your life that you are grateful for – every, last one. It may require you to fill an entire legal pad with the gifts and blessings that God has provided. This exercise serves to shift our focus (or obsession) away from our worries to remind us of God's goodness and grace.

I can be deeply grateful and still be relaxed about the likelihood that challenges will inevitably arise. They may arrive today, next month, or even next year. Regardless, I can rest in the notion that I am still loved by God beyond my understanding. And I can feel a genuine peace of mind in the knowledge that God will equip me to face, and ultimately deal with, these inevitable challenges with faith, patience, perseverance, and with confidence that God can be trusted with my future.

Why would God tell us to *give thanks in all circumstances*, when He knows well the types of hardships we'll face (1 Thes 5:18)? Because giving thanks is a concrete expression of our faith in God and reminds us that our lives are in His hands. And when we do, His promise to us is that we'll experience a freedom and a peace that surpasses all understanding! Gratitude may be the most powerful antidote of all to our propensity to worry!

Pray without ceasing

Excessive worry is convincing evidence that we're operating in a mode of self-reliance. Think about it for a minute – if you genuinely and faithfully believe that God is sovereign and will ultimately make all things work together for good, would you worry about the future nearly as much as you do? Your worry could be an admission that God can't necessarily be trusted with your situation - which is convicting.

God invites us to involve him, through prayer and petitions, into each and every situation, relationship, and decision that we could possibly be involved with: *Do not be anxious about anything, but in every situation, by prayer and petition, with thanksgiving, present your requests to God. 7 And the peace of God, which transcends all understanding, will guard your hearts and your minds in Christ Jesus* (Phil 4:6-7).

He hasn't designed us to operate as independent, self-reliant humans – but as a 'branch' connected to His life-giving 'vine,' if we'll faithfully choose to do so. And when we do, we're promised an extraordinary peace that most find elusive - *You will keep him in perfect peace whose mind is stayed on You because he trusts in You* (Isa 26:3).

The trap we fall into is our natural tendency to think beyond the present and to ruminate, to a fault, on what may happen in the future. It's not healthy and it's also not helpful. God knows what lies ahead of us and promises to walk with us...and we can rest in this knowledge and in His perfect peace.

When we get this right...

We experience joy - regardless of our circumstances. You have the ability to decide today whether you'll worry and be preoccupied by what may happen in the future or whether you'll choose joy, regardless of what lies ahead. "Lord, help me to accept my human limitations and the way you designed us to live one day at a time. Equip me to release into your care my concerns and priorities beyond today. I desire the life you promise that is less complicated and less cluttered - to want what you want for me and to love what you love. Grant in me a heart and a spirit that is content and peace-filled each and every day as I faithfully and joyfully await what You reveal, moment by moment."

Supporting Scriptures:

- *Seek first the kingdom of God, and his righteousness...all these things will be given to you as well. Therefore, do not worry about tomorrow...for tomorrow will worry about itself* (Matt 6:33-34).
- *You will keep him in perfect peace whose mind is stayed on You because he trusts in You* (Isa 26:3).
- *Godliness with contentment is great gain* (1 Tim 6:6).
- *Do not be anxious about anything, but in every situation, by prayer and petition, with thanksgiving, present your requests to God. And the peace of God, which transcends all understanding, will guard your hearts and your minds in Christ Jesus* (Phil 4:6-7).
- *Yet you do not know what tomorrow will bring. What is your life? For you are a mist that appears for a little time and then vanishes* (Jas 4:14).

Mindset #4: <u>Choose</u> Not to Worry!

...it's an imperative, not a suggestion

Discussion Questions

- What topics tend to worry you the most (and why?): The past? The future? Career/work? Children? Health? Finances? Politics? Natural disasters? Marriage? Other Relationships? Or...something else?
- Why is worrying so prevalent today, even for the Jesus-follower?

Specific to the antidotes to worry listed in this chapter:

- Which of your worries are outside of your "circle of influence/concern"?
- How can you better manage your time/calendar to allow you to live more-fully in the present and not worry so much about the future?
- How much do your expectations influence your tendency to worry?
- Why is contentment so elusive in today's consumer-driven, social-media-saturated culture?
- How does our natural sense of entitlement contribute to our fears and worries?
- How can gratefulness minimize our worries?
- And what role does prayer play in all of this?

Recommended Activities

- Identify one significant worry in your life and wrestle with a few questions:
    - Why is this a significant worry?
    - Am I (or anyone) benefiting in any way from the worry?
    - Can I trust God with the outcome on this issue?
    - What is the healthiest, most life-giving mindset I could embrace related to this concern?
- Ask God to reveal to you why your prevalent worries exist and pray for the strength and faith to choose mindsets that releases these worries entirely into His care.

Mindset #5: <u>Choose</u> Humility

...not pride

In today's culture, you'd be hard-pressed to find someone who doesn't fight a daily battle where pride and selfishness compete for control of their lives because most of us live with an overwhelming sense of self-importance. The paradox and the challenge is that we can't really decide that loving God and loving others is our primary calling without a posture of humility. We also won't make much progress on the journey to becoming more Christ-like unless the predominance of our pride and selfishness is extinguished.

Therein lies the struggle to <u>choose</u> humility.

We're here to serve

Let's face it – we're innately tempted to think of ourselves first and foremost. Some argue we're born with this tendency; others contend that it's more of a learned behavior. Regardless, we operate as though we're the center of the universe – at least our version of the universe. And we do so, at least in part, in an attempt to achieve that elusive sense of happiness.

And yet, Harvard professor Arthur Brooks, an expert on the topic of happiness, commonly cites research that proves that humility is actually positively correlated with happiness and life satisfaction.

This may explain why God calls us to a counter-intuitive paradigm...and mindset. Specifically, Jesus implores us, ...*do*

sh ambition. *Rather, in humility, value others*
ᵖhil 2:3).

God and to love others well depends on the
ᵉ're able to <u>choose</u> this mindset of humility.
nking less of yourself; it's thinking about
I our preoccupation with ourselves is usually
liment to prioritizing the needs of others.

I seven deadly sins, "pride" may be the most dangerous and insidious. For the Jesus-follower we'll define pride as an excessive belief in one's own abilities that interferes with our recognition of the grace of God. It's been called the sin from which all others arise – which is why it's so dangerous. When pride is prevalent in us, humility is sparse.

There must be profoundly strategic reasons why the Bible has so much to say on the topic - with over 50 verses in the Old and New Testament combined. Here are two of the most convicting to me:

- *When pride comes, then comes disgrace, but with humility comes wisdom* (Prov 11:2).
- *Jesus called the Twelve* (apostles) *and said, "If anyone wants to be first, he must be the very last, and the servant of all"* (Mark 9:35).

How much clearer could God express the dangers of pride? Or the honor associated with humility? God's Kingdom is literally an upside-down world – *the first shall be last and the servant of all*. And if our aspiration, and God's desire, is for us to become more Christ-like (Mindset #3), pride may be **the** primary stumbling block standing in our way to achieving this end.

Pride is why we don't want to 'give in' in the middle of an argument; it's why we don't like being challenged by our spouses; it's why we pout like adolescents when we don't get our way; it's why we prefer to do things "our way"; and it's why we don't like to admit when we're wrong.

Why, on the other hand, is humility so elusive? Mostly because it requires us to die to our own self-interests. Our selfishness, mostly fueled by our personal pursuit of happiness, is dominant in our activities and our decisions and the notion of giving up control is more frightening to us than walking precariously to the edge of a dangerous cliff.

Genuine humility literally requires us to be 'empty' from an earthly perspective and to be 'filled' instead with the power of the Holy Spirit. Humility asks us to be "less" so that Jesus can be more. And our self-preoccupation resists this mindset almost without consideration.

We're also called to think of others as better and more important than ourselves. This is easy to say, but difficult to genuinely apply because it requires your priorities and desires to become secondary, not primary. It means your "happiness" is not the goal to be pursued; but your righteousness, in God's eyes, is the real pursuit. And when we pursue righteousness, we actually get both.

Humility is what Jesus came here to demonstrate first-hand more than 2000 years ago with the ultimate sacrifice of His own life for our salvation. For the husbands reading this – here's a paradox for you to consider about our 'selective' self-sacrifice mentality: most of us would literally take a bullet for our wives without a second thought and yet, we struggle mightily to treat her with love, kindness and patience on a day-to-day basis. Why the dichotomy?

More importantly, what are we called to do? Paul captures our sacrificial call well:

> Do nothing out of selfish ambition or vain conceit, but in humility consider others better than yourselves. Each of you should look not only to your own interests, but also to the interests of others. Your attitude should be the same as that of Christ Jesus: Who, being in very nature God, did not consider equality with God something to be grasped, but made himself nothing, taking the very nature of a servant, being made in human likeness. And being found in appearance as a man, he humbled himself and became obedient to death— even death on a cross (Phil 2:3-8).

If humility is this important in God's design and creation, what's required of us to embrace and not resist a humble spirit? It requires a healthy and powerful dose of vulnerability...

The power of vulnerability:

Over 50 million people have watched Dr. Brene Brown's Ted Talk™ titled, *The Power of Vulnerability* - a testament to the importance of this topic. She argues that vulnerability, the ability to embrace your true, authentic, and flawed self, is not only healthy for us personally, it's also one of the most endearing qualities that any of us can possess. It's about accepting and loving your imperfect self exactly as you are without shame or apology.

Consider for a minute someone you've met in the past who struggled with some type of addiction. If they were surprisingly open and forthcoming about their addiction and recovery – did it make you respect them more...or less? For most of us, we're immediately drawn to people who are honest and vulnerable. They tend to make us less likely to feel shame about our own sins and struggles. That's the power of vulnerability. It allows us to be far less concerned about what others think and far more comfortable with being 'real.'

The reason we struggle with being real is that our pride insists that we only show the world our best. Not our flaws. Not our fears. Not our weaknesses. And certainly not our failures! Therein lies the problem!

God's design is entirely different. He designed us to be real; to be honest; and to be vulnerable – even, or perhaps especially, when it collides with our innate, prideful nature.

The 'posture' of humility

You and I aren't likely to just wake up one day and *become* humble. I suppose God could orchestrate a supernatural transformation but it seems unlikely and uncommon. The way God often transforms us from innately self-oriented to genuinely others-focused is through adversity.

Some of the most humble people I've met have experienced serious trials in their marriages – and those trials were transformational in their journey from pride-filled to humble. When someone loses their job it's usually humbling because their confidence and sense of financial security are now shaken. Even Alcoholics Anonymous' twelve-steps has a primary tenet: "I am powerless over my addiction and I need some help."

Whether your humility grows because of adverse events or through the transformational power of the Holy Spirit, there are a few common "postures" (or attributes) that are prevalent in genuinely humble people and these postures equip them to thrive with an endearing, humble spirit.

They live for an audience of one – God. As a result, they're far-less consumed by what others may think about them or about their choices and priorities. So often it's our pride that creates our unhealthy preoccupation with how we're perceived by others.

They have an accurate self-assessment – and fully embrace this assessment without shame. They are not overly generous about their strengths, nor overly-critical about their deficiencies.

They recognize that their nature is sinful and that we all fall short of God's glory and design for us. And because of this honest acknowledgement of their flawed nature, they have a profound sense of gratitude for the gift of God's grace and His forgiveness of their sins.

They love God more than they love anything else. And it is God's unconditional love that equips and motivates them to put the interests of others in front of their own self-interests.

All of this sounds great in theory, but what does a genuinely humble person really act like day-to-day? I feel compelled to confess that the list below is aspirational for me. We're all a work-in-process when it comes to humility. And we get countless opportunities each day to test our humility – many of which we fail because of the grip that our self-interest has on us. Nonetheless, here's a few observable behaviors and attitudes of the people we all are privileged to witness and admire who are furthest down the path to humility:

- They don't boast and tend to avoid the spotlight. You'll never see them bragging about their titles, accomplishments or about what they've done and for whom.
- They give others the credit. If something noteworthy is accomplished, they'll always point to the contributions of others rather than their own.

- They're generous – with their money, certainly, but even more so with their time and energy. And they'll do so with anonymity whenever possible.
- Their 'legacy' doesn't matter - because their legacy is all about what **they** did, which is far less important amongst their priorities.
- They love others well, including those they may not know well – or at all.
- They're sensitive to the leading of the Holy Spirit – which is a constant acknowledgement of their dependence on God (vs. their self-reliance).
- They listen a lot more than they talk and they ask great questions of others that makes others feel a genuine sense of interest and care.
- They're willing to admit when they're wrong – and do so quickly and gracefully
- And, there are no tasks that are beneath them because they exude a posture of true servanthood...joyfully.

I know the list above is daunting because it's so counter to what many of us grew up thinking and believing. They're even counter to the culture we live in that screams polar-opposite messages that implore us to think mostly about ourselves and our happiness above all else.

But we've been designed by God in a different, counter-cultural way. Humble followers of Jesus have a deep desire to use their gifts and resources for the benefit of others. When we embrace this mindset of humility, we experience the truly abundant life promised us that provides us with a genuine sense of joy, peace, and purpose.

Humility is a choice we each get to make every day. We can choose to hide the parts of our past and personality that might shine a less glamorous light on us – but we sacrifice living freely. Or, we can adopt the truth that as Christians, we have an audience of one – our Creator God.   When we make that choice, we live free from shame because we're not hiding behind a well-crafted façade.

What about you – what will you <u>choose</u>? Hiding behind an innate pride or enjoying the liberation and freedom that accompany humility and vulnerability? It's a choice we all have dozens of opportunities to make each day as we encounter those God puts in our path.

When we get this right...

It's a transformational and aspirational journey from self-centered to others-centered. "Lord, I often feel powerless to the allure of selfishness. Help me to die to my self-interest and to grow in your call to humility – not thinking less of myself, but equipped and capable of thinking of myself so much less. I take comfort in the knowledge that this can only be done with Christ working in and through me and I look forward to sensing your pleasure and glory as I take small steps toward a humble spirit."

Supporting Scriptures

- *...do nothing out of selfish ambition. Rather, in humility, value others above yourselves* (Phil 2:3).
- *Humble yourself before the Lord and He will exalt you* (Jas 4:10).
- *When pride comes, then comes disgrace, but with humility comes wisdom* (Prov 11:2).
- *Before his downfall a man's heart is proud, but humility comes before honor* (Prov 18:12).
- *Jesus called the Twelve and said, "If anyone wants to be first, he must be the very last, and the servant of all"* (Mark 9:35).
- *My power is made perfect in weakness* (2 Cor 12: 9-10).

Mindset #5: <u>Choose</u> Humility

...not pride

Discussion Questions

- Why is humility so elusive to all of us?
- In your experience, what most often contributes to a person's ability to become more self-less?
- Can you think of people you know well that are genuinely humble?
  - What makes them humble?
  - Provide some examples that illustrate their humility.
- Why is vulnerability an important attribute for humility?
- Review and discuss the "postures" and "attributes" of humility in this chapter – are there others that you would add?

Recommended Activities

- For the next week, consciously look for the subtle ways that your pride and selfish nature are evident. What are your mindsets that are impeding your spirit of humility – i.e., pride, entitlement, etc.?
- Identify 1 or 2 people you admire as genuinely humble – write down the posture and attitudes that make this obvious (and admirable) in them.

- Ask God to equip you with a humble spirit – that loves God above all else and puts the welfare of others above your own.

Mindset #6: <u>Choose</u> Forgiveness

...sooner than later

Forgiveness, or lack thereof, has been more painful for many people than I might have predicted. Specifically, we often struggle to forgive those that have hurt us deeply in the past and unforgiveness has the power to rob us of our joy.

There's little doubt that we've all been hurt by someone's actions or words in numerous ways throughout our lives. It's worth noting though that this goes both ways and we've no doubt hurt others in similar fashion. It's also easy to predict that we'll hurt others and be hurt again in the future because we're all imperfect, self-interested people and conflicts are inevitable. It's often those we're closest to that hurt each other the most!

In a perfect world, you'd get everyone around you to agree that we won't do anything to hurt each other going forward. Forgiveness won't even be necessary! This is far easier said than done of course. Instead, let's accept the reality that we're going to cause hurt and we're going to experience hurt – whether we like it or not!

And when we are hurt by others, we have two starkly different choices: 1) hold on to the hurt and anger at least until the other person says they're sorry - which may take a while and impact you negatively in both the short and long-term; or 2) embrace this Mindset #6 and <u>choose</u> instead to forgive them... sooner than later. The first choice is most common. The second is unquestionably the most beneficial for you and ultimately for others as well.

An author who is gifted on this crucial topic is Lysa TerKeurst who wrote the book, *Forgiving What You Can't Forget.* Her story of hurt and betrayal and the subsequent forgiveness and healing has educated and inspired countless people who struggle with this common challenge.

Her perspective is fairly simple and yet powerful. An immature version of forgiveness, in her view, argues that forgiveness should only be given once we know that the person who has hurt us has apologized and asked for forgiveness. This 'reconciliation' is ideal...in theory.

Practically speaking though, this version is most difficult and damaging to you because often the other person is no longer in your life, doesn't realize they hurt you, or worse yet, doesn't even care about your lingering hurt. When we hold onto our hurt while awaiting an apology and reconciliation, we're mostly hurting ourselves in that process. With this approach, you can't really forgive someone who doesn't seek our forgiveness and our healing is dependent on someone else's actions.

TerKeurst describes the 'mature' version of forgiveness as a process that sweeps the hurt in our heart clean because we don't make our healing dependent on another. "We have to decide that we've suffered enough and unhitch our ability to heal from their choices," explains TerKeurst. "I have carried the weight of suffering and unforgiveness way too long!"

Her principles give us the freedom to separate the act of forgiveness from the act of reconciling the relationship. When you embrace your freedom to forgive without reconciliation when necessary, there's nothing (and no one) precluding your ability to forgive except perhaps the misplaced belief that your lack of forgiveness is somehow harming the person that hurt you – and that's not at all likely.

Forgive others so your Father in Heaven may forgive you

There's another profound and spiritually-significant reason to generously offer forgiveness. The scriptures are consistent as captured in Mark's gospel: *Forgive him so that your Father in heaven may forgive you* (Mark 11:25). Consider the implication of Jesus' words – if we want to be forgiven for our sins, we're called to forgive others. Notice he doesn't include a qualifier about whether or not they deserve our forgiveness!

Even the Lord's prayer reinforces this principle: *Forgive us our trespasses as we forgive those who trespass against us* (Matt 6:12). Once again, there is no qualifier or contingency for forgiveness (i.e., *only if they deserve it*)!

And finally, Paul reinforces the principle when he writes: *Get rid of all bitterness, rage and anger, brawling and slander, along with every form of malice. Be kind and compassionate to one another, forgiving each other, just as in Christ God forgave you* (Eph 4:31-32).

It goes both ways – asking for forgiveness

It's easy to focus on the ways that we've been hurt and the importance of forgiving others in those situations. But we're equally guilty of hurting others, sometimes even without realizing it. And it's often our pride that prevents us from reconciling with those we have hurt or offended.

When we seek forgiveness, it's amazing how quickly it can bring down the 'walls' between us and those that we've hurt. It shouldn't really surprise us because Jesus addressed the issue of reconciling with those we've hurt: *If we confess our sins, He is faithful and righteous to forgive us our sins and to cleanse us from all unrighteousness* (1 John 1:9).

When we're willing to ask for forgiveness, others are all the more likely to ask for your forgiveness and reconciliation becomes far more likely – for the benefit of all. It's your choice entirely.

Remember, the context of our choices in forgiving and asking for forgiveness is Jesus' sacrifice for the forgiveness of our sins – past, present and future sins. When we truly grasp the significance of this gift of grace, we'll have the capacity and maturity to do likewise with others. Make the choice to forgive... sooner than later, with vulnerability and humility and watch how God honors your choices.

Marriage – the forgiveness training ground

The power of forgiveness may be most profound in the marriage relationship because it can reawaken affections you both may have thought were dead. Are you concerned that the affection you and your spouse once cherished is irretrievable because of years of hurt and unforgiveness?

Record keeping between spouses leads to certain death in a marriage. If you apply these same principles (i.e., confession, forgiveness, and reconciliation) to your marriage relationship, your marriage can be renewed and often stronger and more intimately than ever.

Spiritual maturity: forgiving quickly

Paul David Tripp is an author who contends that forgiveness is a matter of spiritual maturity. In his marriage-related book, *What Did You Expect?*, he defines spiritual maturity as the length of time it takes you to forgive the other person when you've been harmed. Is it a few minutes for you...or a few days...or a few weeks?

If it's a few days (or God forbid, a few weeks), why do we retain the anger instead of forgiving and forgetting more quickly? The root cause is often our pride and self-righteousness. Gary

Thomas poses a related question in his best-selling book, *Sacred Marriage*: When you have a conflict in your marriage and you don't know who will be the first to take a proactive step towards reconciliation? He implores, "Perhaps the more mature of you should take that first step." Ouch...does that hit you between the eyes like it does me?

Here's the point of all of this – while our tendency, post conflict, is to withdraw and sulk, partially out of self-preservation and partially because we don't want to say something we'll regret, our spouse interprets our withdrawal as a threat to the relationship's strength and it's damaging to all. The better, more mature alternative is to swallow our pride and our "fairness doctrine" and take Tripp's advice to make the choice to reconcile the conflict...sooner than later as evidence of our Christ-like, spiritual maturity.

"I'm sorry" vs. "I'm wrong"

There are a handful of principles that we highlight in the Marriage Matters workshops I've had the privilege to host (www.menyourmarriagematters.com) for husbands that seemingly turn on a lot of 'lightbulbs' in the minds of most husbands.

One such principle is the difference between saying, "I'm sorry" following a conflict and saying, "I'm wrong". It may sound like a subtle difference initially, but it's far more profound than you may think. Let me highlight the distinction (and admittedly this is coming from a husband that struggles to admit my mistakes and flaws).

When a husband says, "I'm sorry," it can mean one of many things. It could mean:
- "I'm genuinely sorry that I did X (the offense)."
- "I don't know what I did wrong but I'm sorry that you were hurt or reacted negatively."

- Or, "I'm sorry you were hurt but I'm not really remorseful about what I did or why I did it."

Do you see the problem? In all three of these cases (and countless others not listed), your spouse generally perceives that while you're sorry (for *what* may not be clear), she doesn't get the sense that you recognize and accept the responsibility for your part in the conflict. In a strange way, she could easily leave this exchange feeling as though she is to blame for your "being sorry."

There's a better approach to most conflict resolutions but it requires that a spirit of humility be brought to the reconciliation by saying, "I'm wrong" instead of just "sorry." Let's look at the contrast of what it sounds like when we take this alternative approach:

- "I have to confess that I was wrong in the way I …. (fill in the blank)."
- Or, "I'm beginning to recognize that when I do… (fill in the blank) it's not the right way for me to approach this entire issue. Will you forgive me?"

Do you see the difference? The "I'm sorry" examples above have big doses of defensiveness and even subtle accusations towards the other person. The "I'm wrong" statements contain the tone of taking accountability and showing remorse for my actions. And it's the difference in these two tones that makes all the difference in the response and reaction of your spouse (or anyone else for that matter). When we're vulnerable and take responsibility – even if we're not entirely responsible for the conflict/tension – there is usually a profound difference in the way our spouse perceives our heart, our intent and our sincerity.

I have a dear friend who has been married 30+ years who shared this simple principle with his wife following one of our workshops and they both shared with me later that it literally buckled her knees and made her weep because she felt as though her husband finally understood the 'gap' in her mind of what seemed like a lifetime of empty apologies.

But...you may be objecting, "What if I'm not wrong?"

I get it – there are certainly cases where you're not wrong, or perhaps not entirely wrong in creating the conflict. When this is the case, consider two ideas. First, if there are elements of the conflict (including your behavior or reaction) that you could have handled better, own it and say so (i.e., "I know I was wrong in the way I reacted...").

And second, if you genuinely feel as though you weren't wrong in any way, the most vulnerable approach may sound something like, "I don't feel as though I was wrong but I also know that I could have a blind spot on this – can we talk through this so that I can better understand your perspective?" In both of these approaches you are seeking to understand without being either defensive or accusatory. Which is far more likely to lead to reconciliation and to both of your accompanying sense of peace and re-connection.

We're all creatures of habit and one of the habits most of us cling to is holding people accountable for the times we've been hurt. We'll argue, "It's about fairness and equity!", which is logical – except that it assumes that life is designed to be fair and equitable...but 'fair' by whose definition?

Fairness isn't promised to us in the Bible and it isn't realistic in a broken world filled with fallible people (including you and I!). While our righteous attitude seems reasonable, it's our pride and the lack of grace and forgiveness offered to others that has the most negative impact on us – for as long as we choose to hold onto our hurt longer than necessary.

Forgiveness is a <u>choice</u>. It's sometimes a painful one - both granting and asking for forgiveness. Choosing forgiveness doesn't mean we have to forget that we've been injured or that we shouldn't maintain healthy boundaries in the relationships that tend to hurt us the most – we should! It's simply choosing to stop carrying the burden of unforgiveness so that we'll have the opportunity to experience the freedom that comes through forgiveness and in some cases to reconciliation.

When we get this right...

As Christians, we're uniquely called to personify the notion of grace and forgiveness...sooner than later. This is designed by God and for our benefit. "Lord, would you grant me a miraculous desire and ability to forgive those that have hurt me in the past. And give me the courage and humility to ask for forgiveness from those I may hurt - for their benefit and, gratefully, for mine. I recognize that it is my judgmental nature and critical spirit that contributes to my inability to forgive. Strengthen me with your Spirit that equips me to love others supernaturally, not with unhealthy contingencies and provisions."

Supporting Scriptures

- *Forgive him so that your father in heaven may forgive you* (Mark 11:25).
- *And forgive us our trespasses, as we forgive them that trespass against us* (Matt 6:12).
- *If we confess our sins, He is faithful and just to forgive us our sins and to cleanse us from all unrighteousness* (1 John 1:9).
- *Therefore, confess your sins to one another, and pray for one another, so that you may be healed* (Jas 5:16).
- *Do not judge, and you will not be judged. Do not condemn, and you will not be condemned. Forgive, and you will be forgiven* (Luke 6:37).

- *Get rid of all bitterness, rage and anger, brawling and slander, along with every form of malice. Be kind and compassionate to one another, forgiving each other, just as in Christ God forgave you* (Eph 4:31-32).

Mindset #6: <u>Choose</u> Forgiveness

...sooner than later

Discussion Questions

- Why is forgiveness such a prominent topic in the Bible and a common struggle for most people?
- Why is forgiveness so hard to extend to those who've hurt us?
- In your opinion, why was Jesus adamant about the importance of forgiving others?
- Why is forgiving sooner than later a measure of spiritual maturity?
- Why is there a profound difference between "I'm sorry" and "I'm wrong" in reconciling with those we have hurt?

Recommended Activities

- Identify the people in your life (past and present) where lack of forgiveness continues to plague your spirit. <u>Choose</u> to forgive them...for <u>your</u> benefit!
- Pray that God will give you a spirit of forgiveness when you've been hurt, even before you feel it. And for the humility to ask those you've hurt for their forgiveness.

Mindset #7: You're Made for Community

...don't fly solo

Whether you are introverted or extroverted, we are made for relationships. Here's how Arthur Brooks explains this in a recent article published in *The Atlantic*:

> DECADES OF RESEARCH have shown that it is almost impossible to be happy without friends. Friendship accounts for almost 60 percent of the difference in happiness between individuals, no matter how introverted or extroverted they are. Many studies have shown that one of the great markers for well-being at midlife and beyond is whether you can rattle off the names of a few close friends. You don't need to have dozens of friends to be happy, and, in fact, people tend to get more selective about their friends as they age. But the number needs to be more than zero, and more than just your spouse or partner.

In today's culture though, relationships can be compromised by the prevalent political and social tensions that exist. People on all sides of today's spectrum of opinions are downright angry at those that don't agree with their point of view and nobody seems willing to, or even interested in, bridging the divide. Is this tension caused by extreme politics? Or fueled by social media where everyone is entitled to an opinion and they're able to do so anonymously and with minimal accountability?

Dr. Brene Brown delivered a talk at The National Cathedral in Washington DC some time ago and she contended that today's culture is creating a loneliness in most that is deadly – literally!

Here are a few 'headlines' from her talk that are relevant to our final mindset:

- We've sorted ourselves into factions...and we have little interest in intermingling with people who don't think like us.
- There's a direct correlation between the degree to which we've sorted into factions and the levels of reported loneliness...and the faction's members don't really love and care about each other – they just like hating those that don't think like they do.
- This all leads to the highest levels of loneliness this country has ever experienced – which impacts us physically, emotionally, and perhaps especially, spiritually.

In Brown's words, we long to belong, we long to be connected with others and we long to be loved. But today's culture is severing our connectedness. God did not create us to live in isolation. He neurologically wired us to love and care about each other. Brown challenged her audience to, "Come together in community with people you know and even with people that you don't know. We're called to find the face of God in every other human we come in contact with." Could the start of our transition back to civility and connection start with this simple principle?

A cord of three strands is not easily broken

One of my favorite Bible verses is in Ecclesiastes 4 and it contrasts the vulnerability of a cord with only one strand vs. an exponentially stronger "cord of three strands". The author creates the metaphor to help us understand how much better off we are as we walk through life with the benefit of relationships with other people (even one or two close relationships) and with God (the third cord). In essence, we're far better together than any of us could possibly be by ourselves.

God didn't design us to do life alone. From the beginning of God's church in the Book of Acts there were communities of people that did life together – to care for each other, to love each other, and even to support and hold each other accountable when needed.

The challenge and opportunity to embrace this principle is more important today than ever. It's imperative that we proactively endeavor to find one, or better yet, a few, like-minded and faith-filled people with whom we can walk life's journey together. Proactively identify a select few people (or even a couple, for those who are married) with whom you can foster genuine, vulnerable relationships where love and acceptance are unconditional. These invaluable relationships with faith-centered people will provide you wisdom, accountability and care.

I'll confess that this mindset runs counter to my natural introversion. While I've spent much of my adult life acting like I'm an extrovert, I'd far rather read or write at home than be in a room with dozens of people making small talk. I have to be determined and intentionally choose, at times at least, to be around other people so that we can help and care about each other. God designed us for community – both introverts and extroverts!

We've applied this simple philosophy to the Christ Centered Career Groups (www.c3g.org) career search networking organization that we initially started in the Atlanta area in 2003. The premise: we bring together job seekers every Monday morning to facilitate career networking. We've averaged nearly 100 attendees each week (and 13,000+ since we started) with the idea that every job seeker will get back to work faster if we band together, on behalf of each other, for the benefit of all and for the glory of God. It's been inspiring to see God's masterful design in action as these job seekers have forged new, and often lasting relationships.

Numerous studies on longevity and happiness conclude that the primary difference between people who feel a pervasive sense of happiness and those who don't is most often the nature and the strength of a few, deep relationships – not the fleeting comfort of hundreds of "likes" on our most recent social-media posts. It doesn't even have to be very many relationships – just a few that allow you (and the others) to feel a genuine sense of being loved without conditions.

He/She who walks with the wise…

Proverbs is always a reliable source to get clarity on these principles and it reinforces the value of these key relationships in our lives: *Whoever walks with the wise becomes wise, but the companion of fools will suffer harm* (Prov 13:20). The message is clear: forging the right relationships isn't simply spending time with just anybody. Identify and proactively pursue relationships with people who have the potential to make you better, wiser, and more Christ-like. And you, in turn, can invest your time and energy into their lives to allow God to work in and through you for your mutual benefit and for the benefit of those who witness these unique, Christ-centered relationships.

Maximize positive relationships; install boundaries with toxic ones

One final principle worth expanding on is the choice we have to spend time with people who are positive influences in our lives, and correspondingly, *not* with those who aren't. Too often we assume we're "stuck" with certain relationships that seemingly drain the life out of us. Whether they're unkind, needy, or sometimes even abusive – it can sometimes be hard to distance ourselves from these people for numerous reasons. We don't want to hurt them; we worry about what they will think of us; we don't have healthy boundaries in the relationship; we don't know how to say 'no'; and a myriad of other reasons that prevent us from walking away from these unhealthy relationships.

You *do* have a choice. Have the confidence to <u>choose</u> to spend more time with the people in your 'circle' who are helpful, genuine and caring. And, at the same time, have the courage and conviction to <u>choose</u> to spend far less time (or none) with the toxic people in your life who have proven to drain you at the very least, or worse yet, hurt you.

God calls us to love others but He didn't ask us to invest our time and energy into unhealthy relationships. For a more detailed read on this topic – I'd recommend Gary Thomas' book, *When to Walk Away*.

Smartphones – our friend or foe?

As I wrestled with this final mindset focused on the importance of key relationships in our lives, the topic of smartphones – those wonderful, effective, efficient, expensive and yet, awful smartphones nagged me as a topic worth addressing.

There's no question about their potential value. They provide access to useful information – news, articles, podcasts, etc. They give us the ability to communicate and connect with those we work with and even face-to-face virtually with those we love the most in life. They deliver electronic calendars and built-in task-management functions that keep us organized. They even give us the mobility to work from just about anywhere in the world with the help of a high-speed Internet connection. What could possibly be the downside of this great technology?

In truth, these limitless little 'computers' are actually contributing significantly to these loneliness factors and to our discontent in significant ways:

- Well intentioned or not, social media apps like Facebook, Instagram and Pinterest have been designed by their founders to be hyper-addictive and they feed our innate tendencies to compare ourselves with other people. How can this not contribute to today's growing discontentment and our insatiable desire for 'more'?
- The Internet, and the apps and websites we spend most of our time engaging aren't vulnerable or transparent in the least. They're fueled by anonymity because people are able to say whatever they please without repercussions. It's just not real life.
- And, our smartphones are actually impediments to true, face-to-face, interpersonal relationships. We're able to 'act' like we're interacting with other humans as we 'like' and 'heart' and 'thumbs up' the countless posts we scroll through. But our scrolling is compromising the 'real' relationships that most matter. You only have to go to dinner at the average restaurant or sit in an airport terminal and conduct your own informal survey of human behavior to conclude that we're not talking to each other...because we're glued to our smartphones!

What is the call to action? I'll offer two simple ones:

1. Boundaries – If you don't put some boundaries around this 'enabling' technology it will strangle you and 'disable' your relationships. Maybe it's "x" hours/day of use? Or not using it during meals or in the evenings after 7:00 pm? Whatever your choices, decide what your boundaries will be and commit to honoring them – and thereby honoring the people closest and most loved by you.

2. Decide "What really matters?" – This has become a favorite question of mine because when I struggle between choices, even 2 choices I love – like playing golf and spending an afternoon with Devonie – this question makes it incredibly easy to decide how to spend my precious, finite time. Try it – the next time you're tempted to pull out your smart phone at dinner with your family, ask yourself, "What really matters?" in God's realm at this moment. If you're thoughtful, and 'others-centric' in your answer to this question, you won't pull out your smartphone to check it every time it vibrates. You may even stop it from vibrating when you get new messages!

An amazing portion of people in this world are introverted (like me) and for us, the easiest and most comfortable way to go through life is flying "solo." It's often the path of least resistance and it's "comfortable" in a strange way because it's a lot less work and we can't get hurt as easily. But in reality, this final mindset requires us to come out of our solo comfort zone and into meaningful relationships that are worth our time and effort.

Make the choice to invest in a few key relationships with people that you can love well and that will love you well – exactly as you're designed, flaws and all.

When we get this right...

We have the very best opportunity to experience the abundant life that Jesus promises – including our joy, our peace, and our freedom. "Lord, I know you created us to love and to be loved. Would you grant me the capacity to understand your design for love and equip me with the heart and capacity to invest in the best, healthiest relationships that allow me to fully experience community in the way you've designed."

Supporting Scriptures

- *A cord of three strands is not easily broken* (Eccl 4:12).
- *He who walks with the wise, grows wise; The companion of fools suffers harm* (Prov 13:20).
- *He makes the whole body fit together perfectly. As each part does its own special work, it helps the other parts grow, so that the whole body is healthy and growing and full of love* (Eph 4:16 NLT).

Mindset #7: You're Made for Community

...don't fly solo

Discussion Questions

- Are you more introverted or extroverted? How does influence your tendency to 'fly solo' in life?
- How many deep, fully-known relationships have you had in your adult life? In what ways were these relationships valuable?
- Why are we 'better together' than any of us are alone (*a cord of three strands*)?
- How much time and energy are required to develop these special relationships? Why is it worth the investment?
- When you've experienced unhealthy relationships, how have you used healthy boundaries to protect yourself?
- Does your smartphone enhance or inhibit your relationships with those closest to you? In what ways?

Recommended Activities

- Identify one or two people who have the potential to develop into deeper relationships and determine how you could invest in these relationships proactively.
- Join a small group in your church community.
- Ask God to guide your path and connect you with one (or a few) people who you can 'do life' with and glorify God in the process.

Epilogue

There it is – 3 Truths:

1. Our Creator, God is real
2. You are deeply known and loved by God...exactly as you are
3. Jesus is the gift of grace...that secures your freedom, today and eternally

...and 7 Mindsets: (with the "C" words highlighted to help you remember each)

1. God is in **Control**...of the outcomes
2. Our **Calling**: Love God & Love Others... with your skills and gifts
3. Becoming **Christ-like**...is a journey
4. **Choose Not to Worry**...it's an imperative, not a suggestion
5. **Choose Humility**...not pride
6. **Choose to Forgive**...sooner than later
7. You're Made for **Community**...don't fly solo

You may feel, as I do, that some of these are more of a struggle than others. You're also likely pondering a bigger question: If I continue to make progress in embracing these healthy mindsets – what really changes? Do I feel different? Do I think differently? Do I act differently? The short answer is, "Yes."

We tend to go about each day mostly self-absorbed. Our life can seem like the only thing that really matters because we're so consumed by our own activities and priorities. Often this self-preoccupation is the only thing that feels 'real.'

I'm reminded of the fable of the two brick layers working side-by-side who are asked by a passing pedestrian, "What are you doing?" The first worker, whose focus is predominantly on the specific task-at-hand, replies, "I'm laying brick." The second, knowing that his work is part of something much bigger replies, "I'm building a cathedral!" The same work and yet drastically different perspectives.

Are you focused on your own 'brick-laying' or are you part of God's bigger 'cathedral?'

We're all invited to be part of something and someone much bigger than us and our daily tasks. Our ability to keep this broader perspective will be determined by our mindsets. The right mindsets will enable us to experience a pervasive sense of gratitude, contentment and even joyful anticipation of what God is architecting in the world and in our lives.

What changes?

These mindsets equip us to live and thrive in a new and different way. How will it really manifest itself? Here are some examples of how your daily perspectives can change:

- Even if I do face trials and challenges today, I'm really not worried. In fact, I have a joyful anticipation because I fully trust that whatever may come, either planned or even surprises, I have confidence that God will bring good from it all.
- I have a deep sense of gratitude for the countless gifts that God provides – including small, seemingly insignificant gifts – like a warm shower each morning, or having coffee with someone I love, or a soft pillow to set my head on each night – not because I feel entitled to these gifts but because they are truly unmerited gifts!

- I'm deeply satisfied that I am loved by God...exactly as He created me. And secure in my identity in Christ, not in my career or my bank account.
- I can rest in knowing that my calling is simple each day – to love those that God chooses to intersect in my path in small or even large ways. I don't 'wonder' what else God expects of me.
- I'll live each day (and each moment) fully present. Whether in the presence of other people or doing a task on my own, I'm not pre-occupied by past regrets, or future worries – but fully present and fully-invested as though working (and playing for that matter) for the Lord!
- My joy isn't dependent on the perception or reaction of others, because I have fully embraced that I have an audience of one – God. And His love isn't contingent on my performance or my accomplishments.
- I've learned to forgive others generously (and sooner than later) – for my own benefit and peace of mind as God has called me to do.
- I have an extraordinary sense of contentment – grateful for where I am and with whom – not longing for what (and who) I don't have.
- My priorities are amazingly clear and run through the filter of the strategic question, "What really matters?" Asking this question allows me to constantly re-evaluate where I spend my time, money and energy in a way that allows me to love God and love others well.
- I feel a deep sense of hope about the future – because although I don't fully understand so many things, I have faith and trust that eternity with God is unfathomably good! And therefore, I don't have to dread the notion of dying some day because I have confidence in knowing how this story ends!

Jesus came to give us 'life'

The gospel of John is filled with the word "life" because that's what Jesus came into our world to give us:

- *I came that they may have **life**, and might have it abundantly* (John 10:10).
- *Whoever hears My word and believes Him who sent Me has eternal **life** and will not be condemned; he has crossed over from death to **life*** (John 5:24).
- *For God so loved the world that He gave His one and only Son, that whoever believes in Him shall not perish but have eternal **life*** (John 3:16).

Perhaps that's the essence of the one 'word' that we're most missing – **life**. We tend to be preoccupied with our success, our pursuit of happiness, or the accumulation of money and 'stuff,' but we're missing life – at least the abundant life that God miraculously designed for us.

Our preoccupation with worldly pursuits often hinders us from this abundant life. A life where we're fully alive in Christ – not in our own strength; not in our expectations; and not in our desire to control everything in our existence.

Life is a gift. Everyone dies, but not everyone lives. Life isn't about the meaning you create for your own life or the meaning you find in your work and ambitions. You'll find meaning when you recognize that God has given you life and every day is a gift from Him for us to enjoy.

This book captures a relatively short set of mindsets and perhaps all of this sounds overly simple. But if they were simple, an abundant life wouldn't feel so unattainable to so many. Experiencing a deep and sustainable sense of joy, peace, purpose and even freedom – which is where we started this entire book – are desirable endeavors, but it doesn't mean they should be pursued as ends unto themselves. They are more the result of when we do "life" as God intended.

Here's another framework to help in the journey - three key disciplines (or habits) that can help sustain your ability to experience these elusive aspirations:

- **Thinking** – making a dedicated commitment to continuously renewing your mind (and mindsets) because our life's journey is less about what you know and far more about how you think and what occupies your conscious and unconscious mind. *Finally, brothers and sisters, whatever is true, whatever is noble, whatever is right, whatever is pure, whatever is lovely, whatever is admirable—if anything is excellent or praiseworthy—think about such things* (Phil 4:8).
- **Thanking** – our genuine, pervasive gratitude is perhaps the single best antidote to worry, fear, and even to overcoming adverse circumstances. *Be joyful always; pray continuously; give thanks in all circumstances for this is God's will for you in Christ Jesus* (1Thes 5:16).
- **And Loving** – our capacity to love others is dependent on the depth of the love we experience from God. He is our source. *A new command I give you: Love one another. As I have loved you, so you must love one another. By this everyone will know that you are my disciples, if you love one another* (John 13:34-35).

Trust is essential

When I'm asked if there's a way to make all of this even simpler – my answer is, "Yes." Embracing healthy mindsets is mostly about *trust*. You can be successful or you can be struggling; you can be faith-filled or you can have countless doubts; you can be an extrovert or you can be an absolute introvert. Regardless of who and where you are in these spectrums, your peace, joy and purpose are directly correlated to the degree to which you *trust* God.

You can literally <u>choose</u> to trust God with your failures, your finances, your children, your marriage and relationships, your career, and your future. You can even trust God with today's appointments and circumstances.

And when you *really* trust God, you'll do a lot less striving, worrying, judging, and feeling entitled. And you'll be far more apt to be grateful, humble, content, and joyful.

You won't make this choice to trust God unless and until you believe that God is sovereign. You won't make this choice to trust God until you believe that God loves you exactly as you are – flaws and all. You won't make this choice to trust God until you believe that God will make all things work together for good. And, you won't make this all-important choice to trust God unless you genuinely believe that your eternal future is secure in Him.

Peace, joy, purpose, and freedom

We started this book by highlighting a survey that concluded that what the average person most wants more of in life are peace, joy, purpose, and freedom. These aspirations are crucial, transcendent and most-often-elusive. Here are a few uncomplicated perspectives on each:

Peace - is truly a gift from God when we make the conscious choice to genuinely trust Him: *You will keep him/her in perfect peace whose mind is stayed (steadfast) on You because he trusts in You* (Isa 26:3). You'll experience this perfect peace when your mind is less focused on yourself and more 'steadfast' on God.

Joy – is not something we can actually pursue, it's a byproduct of pursuing something bigger than your happiness...like God. It's our spiritual 'buoyancy' because even if our circumstances sometimes take us below the surface of life's 'water,' our trust, gratitude and confidence in God's sovereignty prevails to allow us to joyfully thrive above the surface.

Purpose – in God's realm your purpose is clear and relatively simple: love God and love others (Mt 22:37-39). Consider how liberating this could be for those of us who strive ardently to experience a profound sense of purpose.

Freedom – is entirely about our ability to make choices in our lives. We can make poor choices or we can make healthy choices. I pray that you'll exercise your God-given freedom to embrace these 3 Truths and 7 Mindsets that equip you to deeply and pervasively experience each and every one of these elusive aspirations.

Do you sometimes get discouraged that some of the deep longings in your heart are seemingly unquenchable? We pursue success and achievement. We accumulate plenty of 'stuff.' And even if we have a reasonable degree of success in these pursuits, we still can't seem to fill the "God-sized" hole in our hearts.

Your mindsets represent your best opportunity...or your biggest impediment, to filling that hole. You and I have a decision to make – will you <u>choose</u> Christ-centered mindsets that allow you to experience an abundant life where joy, peace, and fulfillment are deeply experienced and sustained? Or will you be impeded and exhausted by the world's definition of success?

Maybe C.S. Lewis had it right when he wrote, "If we find ourselves with a desire that nothing in this world can satisfy, the most probable explanation is that we were made for another world."

126

When we truly embrace these truths and mindsets, God becomes foremost - not an afterthought. Loving others well becomes *the* priority – not our success and achievement. We're not wrapped up in our own self-interest or in the impression we make on others – but in serving. We grant forgiveness and ask for forgiveness humbly and generously – not harboring our hurts and disdains. And we don't worry about the future or fear what's to come - but rest in the confidence that God is sovereign over all. *That* is where our true joy and peace are derived!

Jesus' invitation and promise is irresistible, *Come to me, all you who are weary and burdened, and I will give you rest* (Matt 11:28).

"Lord Jesus – enable me to embrace these mindsets, or at least the ones I most struggle to embrace so that I can be used in the powerful ways you've designed. I desire to be your vessel and the branch connected to your ever-nourishing vine. I *trust* Your goodness. I trust what You can see that I cannot. I *trust* You with it all."

Epilogue

Discussion Questions

- How will you know when your mindsets are transforming in a healthy, Christ-centered way?
- What do you believe Jesus meant when he said, *I have come to give you life, and to have it abundantly*?
- What does it mean to *really* trust God on a daily basis?
- Are there people who are close to you that would benefit from walking through these principles with you?

Recommended Activities

- Pray that God will give you the clarity and the faith to trust Him in a way that allows you to experience Jesus' promise of the abundant life – filled with pervasive peace, joy, and purpose.

Recommended Reading/Resources

- Lee Strobel's book, *The Case for Christ*
- Stephen Covey's book, *The 7 Habits of Highly Effective People*
- Lysa Teurkurst's book, *Forgiving What You Can't Forget*
- Gary Thomas' book, *When* to *Walk Away: Finding Freedom From Toxic People*
- Bob Goff's book, *Everybody, Always: Becoming Love in a World Full of Setbacks and Difficult People*
- Peter's blog – A Servant's Musings on WordPress https://wordpress.com/view/aservantsmusings.wordpress.com
- Peter's book, website and workshop materials for husbands interested in transforming their marriages – starting with you: www.menyourmarriagematters.com

Made in the USA
Columbia, SC
31 December 2021

53100742R00074